A Study Guide for Small Group Leaders

TITUS

I0141843

A practical guide
for setting up a great church

DON FANNING

Branches
PUBLICATIONS
Pensacola, Florida

First Edition 2014
Titus
Published by
Branches Publications
2040 Downing Dr.
Pensacola, FLA 32505

Branches Publications was started to publish missions and discipleship training tools to equip leaders and teachers to be strategic with their lives by making disciples and fulfilling the Great Commission.
More materials are available at www.tgcresources.com

Other books by Branches Publications can be purchased online at
www.branchespublications.com:

What in the World is God Doing? - An Introduction to Missions
* *Walking His Way: A Daily Devotional Bible Study on the Commands in the NT*
* *Ten Steps of Discipleship*
* *Inductive Bible Study Methods*
* *Romans: A Study Guide for Small Group Leaders*
* *Revelation: A Study Guide for Small Group Leaders*
1, 2, 3 John: Know for Certain
Gifts for Today
* *Spiritual Gifts: A Survey and Definition of the Spiritual Gifts*

* These books are also available in Spanish.

CONTENTS

Introduction

Historical background

Paul had been imprisoned for five or six years ever since his last trip to Israel where the non-believing Jews rejected his intent to help the poor believing Jews with offerings from the Gentile churches. The resulting tumult ended in Paul being arrested and imprisoned three years in Caesarea then a long journey to Rome followed by another 2-3 years of house arrest.

Once Paul was acquitted of trumped up charges of sedition at the end of the Book of Acts, he visited Ephesus and left Timothy there to establish the churches. From there he went to Macedonia (northern Greece) where he wrote back to Timothy his first epistle (1 Tim 1:3).

Evidently Paul teamed with Titus for an evangelistic trip to Crete, an island off the SE coast of Greece. During Paul's journey to Rome as a prisoner his ship had sailed close by the southern coast and stopped for a lengthy stay at a port called "Fair Havens, near the city of Lasea." (Act 27:8 NKJ)

Titus was a Greek believer who had accompanied Paul to Jerusalem (Gal 2:1-2), but Paul refused to force Titus to be circumcised (Gal 2:3-5), which resulted in considerable opposition to the Gentile expansion of the gospel from the Jewish Christians. Titus had served as Paul's messenger to the Corinthian church (2 Cor 7:6-7, 13-14) and was a source of comfort and encouragement for him.

After their evangelistic trip throughout Crete, Paul left Titus to establish the churches throughout the island, while he went to Macedonia, then to Nicopolis in Achaia (southern Greece) (Titus 3:12). This letter was either written from Nicopolis or Macedonia before Paul crossed the Aegean Sea to Troas (2 Tim 4:13), where he was suddenly arrested and taken to Rome and ultimately beheaded.

The date of writing Titus cannot be established with certainty, but was likely between 63-66 AD during Paul's stay in southern Greece at Corinth.

Purpose

Paul, a disciple-maker, mentored his disciples into strategic ministries that fit their giftedness and abilities. His letters to Timothy and Titus gave them the inspired revelation for the foundation and establishing of the churches in biblical teachings and godly living.

In chapter 1 Paul details how leaders are to be examples of a godly life-style (1:5-9). Likewise Paul details the characteristics of false teachers (1:10-16). The goal of the Christian life is to allow the Holy Spirit implanted within the believer to manifest Himself in a transformed life.

Chapter 2 lays out general principles that are to mark the believers at all stages of life as we help each other practice His Word. All believers are to be transformed by "teaching them to obey all things that I have commanded," as Jesus said in Matt 28:20.

Finally, in chapter 3 Paul exhorts the churches to be zealous of good works (3:1, 8, 14) and maintain the unity of the believers around the core values of God's Word.

CHAP

TER 1

THE CHARCTER OF A LEADER

"Paul, a disciple-maker, mentored his disciples into strategic ministries that fit their giftedness and abilities."

TITUS 1

Titus 1
THE CHARACTER OF A LEADER

Introduction (Titus 1:1-4)

Credentials
1:1a "Paul, a bondservant of God and an apostle of Jesus Christ..."

Paul begins his letter with his humblest self-imposed title followed by his most authoritative title in the establishing of the church. He had given himself over as a "bondservant" of God (*doulos*, "metaph., one who gives himself up to another's will those whose service is used by Christ in extending and advancing His cause among men"). James, Peter and Judas introduce themselves in their epistles with this same title.

Reflection: Why would these great leaders pride themselves in being the "slave" of another giving up their personal rights?

Paul, at the same time was chosen to be the "Apostle to the gentiles" (Rom 11:13 and 2 Tim 1:11) and an "Apostle of Jesus Christ," (in the introduction to 1 & 2 Cor, Ephesians, Colossians, 1 & 2 Timothy, Titus) whose chief apostolic function was to be an eye-witness of His resurrection (Acts 1:21-22; 1 Cor 9:1) and he was responsible for laying the foundation of the church (Eph 2:20) with all the biblical knowledge-tools necessary for the "evangelists, pastors and teachers" (Eph 4:11) to use to "keep on building up" the church (1 Cor 3:10-12).

The introduction to his epistles Paul presented his apostolic credentials of authority in the church to motivate the reader to take his writings seriously.

It should be noted, "No one can lay any foundation other than what is being laid" (1 Co 3:11 NET). There are no additional changes or expansions of this foundation continuing to be established. This was the task of the Apostles to complete for the church. We continue to teach what they taught without additions or reductions (Acts 2:42)

Purpose for writing the book

1:1b "according to the faith of God's elect and the acknowledgment of the truth which accords with godliness,"

The phrase "according to the faith" or for the "purpose of the faith" refers to Paul's mission in life to clarify the "faith" for all ages as to what it means and implies. To trust in the "acknowledgment of the truth" is another way of saying, "Faith comes by hearing and hearing by the word of God" (Rom 10:17).

God revealed that man's sinfulness makes him unacceptable to a holy God. Even if a man does a few "good" things he cannot undo the offensiveness to God for every sin he commits. Only by trusting in God's promises for sinners to be made "justified by faith" (Rom 3:28) can we become accepted by God, yet "not because of righteous things we have done" (Titus 3:5). Paul's message is that only by unmerited favor can sinners be saved.

Reflection: Do you understand and trust in the following verses? Can you paraphrase or quote these verses? Here is an easy diagram called the "Bridge Presentation." Learn the verses in the sequence annotated.

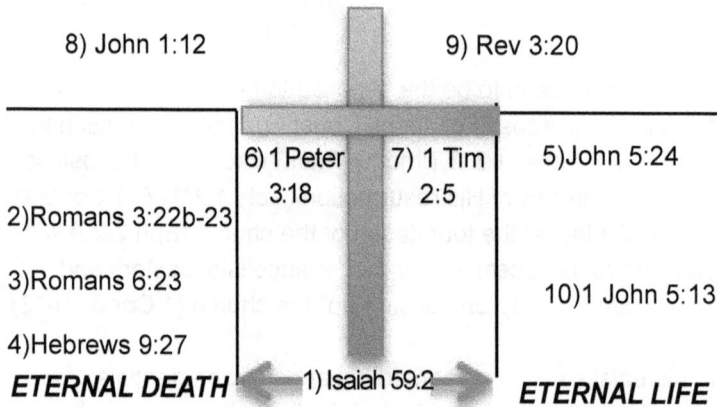

8) John 1:12   9) Rev 3:20

	6) 1 Peter 3:18	7) 1 Tim 2:5	5)John 5:24
2)Romans 3:22b-23			
3)Romans 6:23			10)1 John 5:13
4)Hebrews 9:27			

ETERNAL DEATH ←— 1) Isaiah 59:2 —→ *ETERNAL LIFE*

Those who put their trust in God's promise of forgiveness become "God's elect" or special "chosen" ones as Israel was God's special people in the OT (Deut 7:6; 14:2; Exodus 19:5), thus believers, even Gentile believers, now become the people of God. In a mixed church of Gentile and Jewish believers it was important to establish the acceptance of all Gentile believers as an equal part of the family of God.

"The acknowledgement of the truth," if understood correctly, "accords with godliness" means correct knowledge of truth will result in a godly lifestyle. This is the meaning of the transformation of the believer beginning in the mind or understanding then expressing itself outwardly as Paul wrote, "do not be conformed to this world, but be transformed by the renewing of your mind," (Rom 12:2).

As the mind changes its perspectives about truth, values and priorities, one's practical life transforms to match the transformed mind. A new reality or world-view inevitably works its way out in our attitudes and behavior.

Reflection: How has the gospel changed my daily life and values?

God's eternal plan (1:2)
1:2 "... in hope of eternal life which God, who cannot lie, promised before time began,"

The knowledge of God's plan to redeem [or "pay for"] all man's debt of sin gives every believer a sure "hope of eternal life." This "hope" is not a dream or imagination of a better life, but is grounded on the faithfulness of God, "who cannot lie." "Eternal life" [lit., "life of the eternities"] is our present possession (1 John 5:12).

He promised, "I tell you the solemn truth, the one who hears my message and believes the one who sent me has eternal life and will not be condemned, but has crossed over from death to life. (John 5:24 NET). Faith is taking Christ at His word, because He is trustworthy.

In Greek mythology, the beliefs of the Cretans, the gods often deceived people, which explain why the Cretans were known to be dishonest (Titus 1:12). We become like the God (or gods) we worship.

The only true God of eternity planed how His sinful creation could be made ready for eternity with Him. He promised that He would do whatever it took, even though

11

it cost the suffering and life of God's only Son, Jesus Christ.

Reflection: Does your confidence in God's trustworthiness in His promises give you perfect peace about your eternity?

The eternal plan revealed (1:3)
1:3 "... but has in due time manifested His word through preaching, which was committed to me according to the commandment of God our Savior;"

"In due time" reflects God's perfect timing in bringing to each believer an understanding of His plan for salvation. No one hears and understands the gospel by coincidence. It is made evident or "manifested" to individuals "through preaching" (*kerugma*, "a proclamation, public crier").

It refers to someone who went through the streets of a town giving the news of special events. This is how the gospel spreads: someone announcing the "good news" of Christ's salvation to needy sinners.

This eternal plan from eternity past, which is the only hope for mankind, was entrusted to finite human messengers to propagate. Paul was awe struck by the significance of his responsibility, as we should be as well.

To be a player in God's eternal plan has a sense of majesty to it. Especially when one recognizes how undeserving and unworthy one is to be entrusted with such a global task.

Paul's role was unique in that he entered the ministry under "the commandment of God our Savior." He was not appointed, voted on, or volunteered. He had no choice in the matter of preaching the gospel.

Much of what we know of the gospel is because of His obedience to this command. He told king Agrippa, "I was not disobedient to the heavenly vision" (Act 26:19). By this authority he would train and appoint other leaders to carry on the proclamation of the gospel after him.

The phrase "God our Savior" is an expression of trust and dependency that is used by Paul, Peter (2 Peter 1:1) and Jude (1:25). Paul used it in 1 Tim 1:1; 2:3; 4:10; Titus 1:3, 4; 2:10, 13; 3:4. Paul and Peter identify "God our Savior" as the person of Jesus Christ in Titus 1:4; 2:13; and 2 Peter 1:1.

These are some of the clearest declarations of the deity of Christ. He is the single manifestation of the "invisible" God (Col 1:15 and 1 Tim 1:17).

Reflection: Do I have a strategic sense of how important my role is for spreading the gospel? What am I willing to do about it?

The recipient (1:4)
1:4 "To Titus, a true son in our common faith: Grace, mercy, and peace from God the Father and the Lord Jesus Christ our Savior."

Titus had been an invaluable companion of Paul for a number of years in evangelism and discipling ministries from before and throughout his years of imprisonment in Caesarea and Rome, and now in this evangelistic, church planting thrust on the island of Crete.

Paul called Titus a "son in our common faith," implying that Paul had led Titus to Christ and taught him all aspects of their "faith held in common." The emphasis is on the fact that Paul [a Jew] and Titus [a Gentile] shared the exact same saving faith without distinction (Jude 3).

"Grace" refers to the unmerited favor God gives to undeserving sinners, which Paul desires for the recipient of this letter. "Peace" is the unimpeded and uncontroversial bond between two persons as a result of the resolution of all conflict between them.

The source of these blessings comes "from God the Father and the Lord Jesus Christ our Savior." Paul had just referred to "God our Savior," (1:3) and now uses the same terminology to refer to Jesus as "our Savior." The two are one in the same.

Reflection: If we are all commanded to "make disciples" (Matt 28:19) like Paul did to Titus, what are we doing to make our disciples? This is not just the responsibility of pastors, but everyone of us.

Leadership priority (Titus 1:5-16)

Two-fold delegated assignment (1:5)
1:5 "For this reason I left you in Crete, that you should set in order the things that are lacking, and appoint elders in every city as I commanded you—"

After an indefinite period of evangelistic meetings throughout the island of Crete Paul departs for another outreach leaving his protégé and co-worker, Titus, to "set in order the things that are lacking" among the groups of disciples scattered throughout the island. They obviously had uncovered a number of problems in the churches that Titus was commissioned to resolve.

Cretans were present on the day of Pentecost (Acts 2:11) and some may have responded to Peter's message and been baptized (Acts 2:14). It can be presumed that some of them may have returned to Crete to share the gospel thirty years before Paul's visit.

With little training and fierce Jewish opposition to Gentile Christians everywhere these early believers may have been limited to small groups of unorganized disciples.

Paul's brief trip was both a survey trip and a campaign, but assigning Titus to "set in order the things that are lacking" effectively extended the ministry. There were several problems that needed attention. With no clearly defined leaders to take responsibility for the churches the young believers could easily be persuaded to follow teachers in their false teachings.

Reflections: Why do you believe that leaders of disciples are necessary? Are we responsible for each other?

Qualifications for church leaders and goal of spiritual maturity

This listing in Titus of 17 qualities is similar or identical to the 15 qualities listed in 1 Timothy. Family matters are mentioned first, followed by five management techniques to be avoided, concluding with six virtues to incorporate into their lives.

Titus is more directive than Timothy (i.e., he was ordered to "appoint elders"), where Paul merely lists the qualifications of bishops/elders.

Paul used the term "bishop" or overseer in 1 Timothy (3:1) and two terms interchangeably in Titus: "elder" (1:5) and "bishop" or overseer (1:7) referring to the same group of leaders. The over arching title of these functions is called "pastor" in Ephesians 4:11, a term that refers to the concept of a shepherd caring for his sheep and protecting them while leading them to adequate food or pastures.

"Overseers" are to "shepherd" or "pastor" the "church of God which He pur-chased with His own blood" (Acts 20:28).

The responsibilities of these elders/overseers/pastors is seen as

- Directing the organization and ministries
- Teaching and preaching (1 Tim 5:17)
- Equipping all believers for their gifted ministry (Eph 4:12)
- Shepherding and guarding the church (Acts 20:28-31)
- Leading by example (1 Pet 5:1-4)
- Anointing with oil and praying for the sick (James 5:14).

Essentially, this recognition is for people who desire to serve the church (1 Tim 3:1). Generally they are already doing works of service and now will be recognized officially to broaden and endorse their continuing ministry.

Reflection: Whom do you know that is volunteering to serve the people of God even though they may not be officially recognized? Would you like to follow him?

Qualifications
1:6a "if a man is blameless, the husband of one wife, having faithful children not accused of dissipation or insubordination."

General qualification

"Blameless" – This is someone who "cannot be called into account for or is unreproachable," or "above reproach," but this does not mean perfect or faultless. This is someone who would not be open to attack or accusations in his Christian or secular life. It is a general term for "unquestioned integrity." It is a person who could and should be imitated by others. The term is used for other church leaders as well (1 Tim 3:10) and a synonym in 1 Tim 3:2.

Reflection: What responsibility do these verses below place on leaders? On teachers? On husbands?

John 13:15

Heb 13:7

1 Tim 4:12

Family qualifications

Putting someone into a leadership role is always a little risky. How will he lead once he is given the position? People generally do not change their character, but stress is a good revealer of who we really are. As he is in one situation he will behave in another.

The best test of a leader is how he leads his family. It is declared, "But if someone does not know how to manage his own household, how will he care for the church of God?" (1Tim 3:5 NET) The way he leads in one area will be similar in the other.

"Husband of one wife" – The phrase literally is "a one woman man" that has a number of interpretations, but historically the Jewish Christians may have had multiple wives, but the Christian leaders could only have one wife.

Likewise, the implied characteristic is marital fidelity and moral integrity, especially regarding the opposite sex. This assumes that the church leaders are married, though the same moral and sexual purity would be applicable to an unmarried elder.

That these requirements are not absolute (i.e., must be married) is evident by the same token that it is not required that the man be eliminated with less than two children in the next requirement would indicate. Above reproach in this area is vital so that the gospel is not slandered by a poor reputation.

Reflection: What steps do I take to make certain that my moral integrity regarding the opposite sex is never in question?
"Having faithful children" – Learning oversight must begin at home. The word "faithful" could also be translated "believing children" (as translated in the ESV, NAU).

Paul is reasoning that if a leader is unable to persuade his children to believe, how could he influence others to trust Christ in the ministry? It is not required that he must have children, but if he is "having" children that they be believers.

"Not accused of dissipation or insubordination" – If he has believing children, they must not be "accused of dissipation" ("prodigality" or "incorrigibleness" or "riotous living"). The term is used for "drunkenness" (Eph 5:18) and is associated with pagan practices (1 Pet 4:4), thus not guilty of "sensuality, lusts, drunkenness, carousals, drinking parties" (1 Pet 4:3). The term is used of the prodigal son who "squandered his wealth in wild living" (Luke 15:13).

The term "insubordination" means "undisciplined, disobedient, rebellious, or unruly." It must be emphasized that Paul is not asking more of the leaders than is expected of the children of every Christian family. However, a man must be successful here to be considered for leadership.

Whether fair or not, undisciplined children destroy the credibility of the gospel and the church. The term "children" is not defined but generally applies to minors who remain under the supervision of their parents in their home. Others may need to decide this issue for the sake of the gospel and respect for the testimony of the church.

Reflection: Do you think this restriction is fair? Why?

Management skills
1:7 "For a bishop must be blameless, as a steward of God, not self-willed, not quick-tempered, not given to wine, not violent, not greedy for money,"

Interchangeable use of titles

Paul now uses the term "bishop" whereas he started the discussion about establishing "elders" (1:5) in every city, as he did in Acts 20:17, 28 where he called the "elders" together (20:17), then addresses them as "bishops" (20:28) telling them to do the work to "shepherd the flock" (i.e., to "pastor"). These are not distinct offices but the same position with a different focus.

Titus was now to search for men free of habits or attitudes that would undermine the credibility of the gospel message. Some of them may have required a time of testing. Paul wrote Timothy about deacons, "But let these also first be tested" (1Tim 3:10). He did not indicate how to recognize these traits, but Paul trusted Titus' wisdom.

"Blameless as a steward of God"—The reason for "blameless" is "since he is" a "stewardship" or management skill and leadership of God's people. The following lists describe what is not to be characteristic of a leader/manager of God's people.

Peter lists these skills first as a negative trait followed by the positive trait: "nor as being lords over those entrusted to you, but being examples to the flock; (1Pet 5:3). The way a person manages a business or other organization will indicate his leadership ability in the church. It will not be any different. He must not be accused of the following:

Five leadership vices to avoid

"Not self-willed" – The word means "self-pleasing, arrogant" or "overbearing." This kind of leader disregards the needs of others, stubbornly pushes his own agenda, considers his opinion the only valid one, and seldom listens to anyone's contrary viewpoint.

Sadly, some people want "strong" leaders who are decisive and determined as in the secular world. What is admired in successful businesses may be contrary to these principles.

Biblical leadership is radically different from secular leadership as Jesus taught His disciples, as when He said to them, "You know that those who are considered rulers over the Gentiles lord it over them, and their great ones exercise authority over them. Yet it shall not be so among you; but whoever desires to become great among you shall be your servant." (Mar 10:42-43)

"Not quick-tempered" – The word means "prone to anger" or one who gets irate with others and maintains his anger for a long time, usually holding grudges or anger toward offending people for a long time. Some believe that if you are not harsh or don't get angry no one will fear you. If they are not afraid of you they will not follow what you say, but this tactic is not biblical.

Reflection: What does the following verse have to do with this requirement: "For human anger does not accomplish God's righteousness" (James 1:20 NET)?

"Not given to wine" – This means, "overindulging in alcohol" or "sits a long time alongside wine," thus "drunkenness." This is a concern again for the reputation of the church and the name of Christ that the elder/pastor is to represent.

Some feel that total abstinence from any alcohol is the wisest conviction: "Wine is a mocker, strong drink is a brawler, and whoever is led astray by it is not wise." (Prov 20:1)

"Not violent" – This is a word that means a "striker; hence pugnacious person, bully, quarrelsome person" or "contentious." This is often a tactic of manipulation to get people to be afraid of opposing him: "A violent man entices his neighbor, and leads him in a way that is not good." (Pro 16:29).

A good way to "test" this kind of a person is to correct him and see how he reacts: "A fool despises his father's instruction, but he who receives correction is prudent." (Prov 15:5). Becoming defensive at every correction often leads to anger issues and violent reactions.

"Not greedy for money"—This is one word in Greek, meaning someone who loves money, "the root of all evils. Some people in reaching for it have strayed from the faith and stabbed themselves with many pains." (1Tim 6:10 NET)

Peter included this restriction in his list of vices because it is a dangerous temptation (1 Tim 6:9-10). Jesus taught that when a person seeks to serve money, he cannot serve God (Matt 6:24).

On the other hand, Paul taught the right of those working in the church should be paid a fair salary (1 Tim 5:17-18), but not to the extent that he uses his position for personal advantage abusing the church. This is not referring to a fair profit or good salary, but to what a person will do to always gain the advantage for himself.

These vices of pride, anger, the desire for drink, dominance or wealth can lead a person to stray from the truth and godliness. Anyone who is controlled by any of these vices should disqualify him from the position of elder/overseerer/pastor.

Reflection: What did Jesus mean when he said, "No one can serve two masters, for either he will hate the one and love the other, or he will be devoted to the one and despise the other. You cannot serve God and money." (Mat 6:24 NET)?

Seven Virtues to be evident
1:8 "... but hospitable, a lover of what is good, sober-minded, just, holy, self-controlled,"

Peter drew a distinction between our salvation and the Christian life. Salvation is to trust in the "exceedingly great and precious promises" that have enabled all believers to be made "partakers of the divine nature" (2 Peter 1:4).

The Christian life then is to "make every effort to add to your faith excellence, to excellence, knowledge; to knowledge, self-control; to self-control, perseverance; to perseverance, godliness; to godliness, brotherly affection; to brotherly affection, unselfish love." (2 Pet 1:5-7 NET).

Peter's seven characteristics, which will take "every effort to add to your faith," are comparable to Paul's list of virtues in Titus 1:8. These traits will not come automatically to the Christian life even with the Holy Spirit, but must be added to one's character by diligent discipline.

"Hospitable" – This word literally means "lover of strangers" where travelers in the 1st century would need places to stay for a night or two. Inns were notorious, dirty and expensive. This characteristic reveals a generous and caring spirit of a leader.

"Lover of what is good" – This is one word meaning "loving goodness" both esthetic and practically efficient. This refers to things and people. A Christian leader must reject exposure to whatever is unwholesome and evil, but cling to what is good and wholesome.

Reflection: How would you test someone for obedience to Phil 4:8-9?

"Sober-minded" – This is the word for "self-controlled," which means to "curb one's desires and impulses… temperate," or "to be sensible, or keeping a level head" in the midst of confusion and chaos. Paul must have felt this characteristic was especially needed among the Cretans because he mentions it five times in Titus (1:8; 2:2, 5, 6, 12).

"Just"—This is a word that has a broad meaning for those who make every effort to keep the commands of God or conform to the will of God. They practice what they preach. More obviously this word can refer to "rendering to each his due… passing just judgment on others, whether expressed in words or shown by the manner of dealing with them." (STRONG). John gives this virtue as a sign of genuine conversion: "the one who practices righteousness is righteous" (i.e., "just") (1 John 3:7)

"Holy" -- The word means to be "unique, set apart for a specific function or for God." This characteristic is revealed by his strong inner desire to please God and play a part in God's purpose. This is someone dedicated to God's will.

"Self-controlled"— The leaders must be "disciplined" to resist the wrong and practice what is right. This is one of the characteristics of the fruit of the Spirit (Gal 5:23). The filling of the Spirit is evident by demonstrating self-control or restraint especially when others around him are in panic, fearful or reactionary.

In 1 Cor 9:25 Paul uses the analogy of the athlete who "exercises self-control in all things" as an appeal to Christians in general. Leaders must exemplify the virtues they seek to teach and promote.

Reflection: How would you see the focus of these last three qualities? Which one focuses on others?

Which one focuses on self?

Which one focuses on God?

Skill in the ministry

1:9 "holding fast the faithful word as he has been taught, ..."

This characteristic is acquired by having "been taught" and now has held "fast the faithful word." This has to do with unwavering commitment to the precepts, promises and commands of the unfailing Word of God. Paul described the strategy of the ministry is first to be taught God's Word, then entrust the teachings "to faithful men" who can then teach it to other faithful men (2 Tim 2:2).

Peter wrote that if you have a speaking gift then "let it be with God's words." (1 Pet 4:11[NET]) Regardless of what others say, or if more popular ideas surface, or threats discourage fidelity, this person will never vary from faithfulness to God's Word "as he has been taught."

This is an individual who has gone through a specialized training program in the Word and has learned both how to study the Scripture to discover the grammatical, linguistic and contextual meaning on which he has build the elements of biblical theology.

The test of this characteristic can be measured by how he can answer questions about theology and give biblical responses to case study situations.

Reflection: How can we develop these kinds of men of God according to these verses?

1 Tim 4:6

1 Tim 4:11

1 Tim 4:13

1 Tim 4:15

1 Tim 4:16

1 Tim 5:17

Primary duty
1:9b "... that he may be able, by sound doctrine, both to exhort..."

The personal commitment and practice of God's word to his life qualifies him to confront, exhort and apply God's word to the lives of others. "Sound doctrine" translates the word *hugiaino* from which we have the English word *hygienic*. The idea is to be healthy and wholesome by staying true to the meaning of the original text of the NT.

Deviant teachings bring a multitude of unhealthy consequences. Paul told Timothy, "Hold to the standard of sound words that you heard from me and do so with the faith and love that are in Christ Jesus." (2 Tim 1:13 NET) Staying true to the written Word of God as it is exposited and taught is key to staying healthy spiritually and effective in the ministry.

Ezra was a great example of a faithful pastor as he "set his heart to study the law of the Lord, and to practice it, and to teach His statutes and ordinances"(Ezra 7:10). This kind of a leader will "preach the word; be ready in season and out of season; reprove, rebuke, exhort, with great patience and instruction" (2 Tim 4:2).

This is the task of a leader of God's people. To varying degrees everyone should be preparing to live this way. Those who excel should become the mentors and trainers of everyone else.

Secondary duty
1:9c "... and convict those who contradict."

The word "convict," *elegchein*, refer to "refute, convince and convict." A positive outcome of this rebuke is always the goal (2 Tim 2:25-26) with those who "contradict" or "who speak against" the sound teachings just mentioned. This is an ability to defend and prove your teachings (1 Tim 6:3, 20).

With this background God's man will be able to "exhort and convict those who contradict" because of his personal knowledge and assurance of God's Word. Pastors and teachers have an obligation to clarify the Word of God to create sufficient understanding and discernment to protect them from error and false teachings that distort God's Word.

The word for "convict" means to "refute, generally with a suggestion of shame, to expose, to find fault with, or correct." God's people need to hear and know the erroneous teachings that infiltrate the minds of believers unknowingly.

Paul warned the elders of the church at Ephesus, "I know that after I am gone fierce wolves will come in among you, not sparing the flock. Even from among your own group men will arise, teaching perversions of the truth to draw the disciples away after them." (Act 20:29-30 NET) Unless the church is well trained in God's Word this is inevitable.

Erroneous and false teachers come under various disguises. They use the same Bible, but twist its meanings to create new doctrines. The word "contradict" means to "speak against, decline to obey, declare one's self against him or refuse to have anything to do with him." To contradict God's Word is the same as denying the deity of Christ or the resurrection of Christ.

When doctrines contradict each other, some one is in error and must be corrected. The responsibility of the leader(s) of God's people must be to denounce erroneous and false teachings, fully "speaking the truth in love" (Eph 4:15). The confidence to be this bold demands a deep conviction and clarity of what God's Word is saying.

This is the reason for the required ability to be "able to teach" in 1 Tim 3:2 with the guidelines for this ministry in 2 Tim 2:24-26.

Reflection: Do I know God's Word, or even part of it, sufficiently to recognize deviant teachings and am I able to defend what it says? Do I want to know the Bible well enough to recognize false teachings?

Characteristics of false teachers
1:10 "For there are many insubordinate, both idle talkers and deceivers, especially those of the circumcision,"

Titus was given the task of preparing the churches to recognize and refute the false teachings and immoral living of infiltrators into the churches. Such deceivers had to be stopped or disharmony and chaos would be inevitable.

Paul had written to Timothy, "instruct certain men not to teach strange doctrines, nor to pay attention to myths and endless genealogies, which give rise to mere speculation rather than furthering the administration of God which is by faith," (1 Tim 1:3-4). Human error is inevitable, but false concepts must be corrected for the unity of the body of Christ.

Paul says a number of things about the false teachers in Crete, but does not describe them specifically, though they are primarily from a Jewish background and bring with them legalistic tendencies to corrupt the gospel and the church. Timothy in Ephesus faced similar false teachers that Paul wrote about in 1 Tim 1:3-11. They oppose Paul's teachings revealed to him by Jesus (1 Cor 14:37), rather seeking a Jewish asceticism already in the church at Colossae (Col 2:16-17, 20-23).

The churches on Crete were facing "many insubordinate" teachers who contradicted the inspired teachings of Paul. The word "insubordinate" means, "cannot be subjected to control, or disobedient." They recognize no authority but themselves.

Timothy was facing similar when he was warned, "Now the Spirit explicitly says that in the later times some will desert the faith and occupy themselves with deceiving spirits and demonic teachings, influenced by the hypocrisy of liars whose consciences are seared." (1Ti 4:1-2 NET) The "latter times" were just beginning and have continued throughout the history of the church. When such teachings are uncorrected they bring a multiple of negative consequences.

Reflection: If Paul is insisting on certain characteristics of godly leaders (as opposed to false teachers) what are the opposite characteristics of 1:6-7 that would describe these teachers?

These false teachers were "idle talkers," referring to their ability to persuade and captivate an audience while saying nothing significant. They twist the Bible references out of their context to appear spiritual and biblical while focusing on their experiences, speculations, visions and imagination. They are also "deceivers" appearing to be super spiritual and always able to attract an audience.

Timothy was warned that some believers "will not endure sound doctrine; but wanting to have their ears tickled, ... will accumulate for themselves teachers in accordance to their own desires; and will turn away their ears from the truth, and will turn aside to myths" (2 Tim 4:3-4)

Reflection: How does Peter describe the false teachers he confronted in 2 Pet 2:18?

Legalistic teachers

The major problem was "those of the circumcision" though not exclusively. These were the Jews within the church, sometimes called "Judaizers" because they sought to impose the Jewish legalism and the man-made rabbinical traditions to be spiritual, as well as the OT ceremonial standards.

Reflection: What does Gal 2:11-12 tell us about how Peter learned the seriousness of opposing false teachers?

About fifteen years earlier at the Council of Jerusalem (AD 49, Acts 15), "certain ones of the sect of the Pharisees who [said], 'It is necessary to circumcise them, and to direct them to observe the Law of Moses'" (Acts 15:5). Peter, the lead Apostle in Jerusalem, asked, "Why do you put God to the test by placing upon the neck of the disciples a yoke which neither our fathers nor we have been able to bear?" (Acts 15:10).

The issue was resolved once and for all with the summation of James, the head pastor of the Jerusalem church, saying that they "not trouble those who are turning to God from among the Gentiles, but ... write to them that they abstain from things contaminated by idols and from fornication and from what is strangled and from blood." (Acts 15:12-20). Everyone agreed and the Gentile churches were informed.

However, to demonstrate how "insubordinate" they were, for years the Judaizers persisted in their man-made legalistic approach to being a Christian, rather than simply following the precepts of the NT revelations. In the Cretan churches this error persisted: "Jewish myths and commandments of men who turn away from the truth" (Titus 1:14).

The principle of recognizing false teachings of all sorts and opposing them is indicated by the generic, non-specific nature of the description of their heresy.

Reflection: Have you ever heard people talk strange doctrines or attempt to get people to believe doctrines contrary to the gospel message of God's grace?

Silencing of false teachers

1:11 "...whose mouths must be stopped, who subvert whole households, teaching things which they ought not, for the sake of dishonest gain."

It appears that these false teachers were not speaking during the formal gatherings of the believers, but were isolating distinct families ("whole house-holds") to propagate their false teachings.

In larger groups of disciples their false teachings would be more likely recognized and quenched. This is the practice of many cults which seek to approach individuals or single families to entrap weak believers and to sell them their books.

They create this havoc by "teaching things they should not." These "things" are not detailed but must involve "Jewish myths" and "commandments of those who turn from the truth" (1:14). Paul described some of the teachings at Ephesus by false teachers as prohibitions of marriage and abstinence from certain foods in 1 Tim 4:1-3. It is likely that Paul had much more in mind and left it open ended for future situations.

The idea of "for the sake of dishonest gain" or "dishonorable, disgraceful or shameful" profit, is doing business with the church without authorization of the leadership or intentionally to deceive. Manipulating people for personal profit seems to have been their motive.

Reflection: Why would some think that by pretending to be godly there could be financial profit? (1 Tim 6:4-5)

Has anything changed concerning this issue in 2000 years?

1:12 "One of them, a prophet of their own, said, 'Cretans are always liars, evil beasts, lazy gluttons' "

The reference is to an ancient Cretan poet, Epimenides, a Greek intellectual from the 6th century BC described the reputation of the Cretans as they were known. An illustration of their deception was the tale that the "immortal" Greek god Zeus was buried on their island. They made a verb of their name, "to Cretanize," which was a figure of speech for lying.

The idea behind the phrase "evil beasts" referred to living like animals responding to sensual appetites and passions. Their savageness and violence were the exact opposite of how the Spirit would transform their lives.

As "lazy gluttons" the Cretans had no work ethic and yet loved to eat. One author wrote, "They were self-indulgent, greedy, lustful, overfed, and perhaps in poor physical condition. Paul affirmed that the six-hundred-year-old testimony of Epimenides about the Cretans was still true." (MacArthur, 1960, 60).

Reflection: If this were a true description of a people or community today, How would you begin the ministry among them?

Correction of false teachers
1:13 "This testimony is true. Therefore rebuke~~ them sharply, that they may be sound in the faith,"

If these attitudes entered the church it would self-destruct before it ever began. The "rebuke" ("overthrow, overturn, destroy or subvert") a present tense command means, "be continually rebuking." The adverb "sharply" means to "severely, harshly or abruptly." The root word of the verb means, "to cut" as with a knife or ax. The rebuke was to be decisive and surgical.

There was to be no confusion about what is true and what is false teaching. Timothy and Titus had learned to "reprove, rebuke, and exhort with great patience and instruction" (2 Tim 4:2), while at the same time "The Lord's bond-servant must not be quarrelsome, but be kind to all, able to teach, patient when wronged, with gentleness correcting those who are in opposition, if perhaps God may grant them repentance leading to the knowledge of the truth" (2 Tim 2:24-25).

Reflection: How do you balance the sharp rebuke with the not-quarrelsome attitude, gentle correction and being "kind to all"?

Warning of false teachers
1:14 "... not giving heed to Jewish fables and commandments of men who turn from the truth."

The phrase "not giving heed" is "to bring near" as a ship comes home to port or "to give continual attention to" or "hold or cleave to something." The idea is to not devote oneself to a false idea.

"Myths" are captivating stories of exaggerated events, miracles and supernatural encounters that will cause people to "turn away from hearing the truth" (2 Tim 4:4). The Bible will not seem as interesting as the myths.

Everyone is trying to prove something by stories of phenomena that are claimed to be signs of the supernatural God. Paul wrote to Timothy, "But reject those myths fit only for the godless and gullible, and train yourself for godliness" (1 Tim 4:7 NET).

Reflection: Would you prefer stories of miracles and supernatural events or the study of a passage from the Bible? Be honest.

Which will do you the most good?

The "commandments of men" are made-up rules of spirituality that provoke severe criticism when violated. A critical judgmental spirit is first symptom of legalism. Rules in the North American culture like having to wear a tie on Sunday, women must wear skirts always, no cussing or sports allowed on Sunday, etc., all of which can evoke a false sense of superficial spirituality and self-righteous superiority.

Paul did not specify a specific heresy, so that later readers could apply these general principles to all deviations from God's word or additions to it. The commands in Scripture are general or generic forcing the reader to make personal decisions for how he wants to practice them as to the Lord, not to please men.

Whenever the motive in the disciple's heart is to impress men with their spirituality, be accepted by others or demonstrate submission to man's legalism, the false teachings have surfaced again under a different disguise.

Reflection: What do you consider legalistic teachings that you have heard taught?

Characteristics of false teachers of all ages
1:15 "To the pure all things are pure, but to those who are defiled and unbelieving nothing is pure; but even their mind and conscience are defiled."

In Luke 11:37-41 Jesus was invited to lunch with a Pharisee. When Jesus entered to begin the lunch reclining on the floor he did not follow the ceremonial washing before the meal. The Pharisees were shocked.

Jesus said to them, "'Now you Pharisees clean the outside of the cup and of the platter; but inside of you, you are full of robbery and wickedness. You foolish ones, did not He who made the outside make the inside also? But give that which is within as charity, and then all things are clean for you' " (Luke 11:37-41).

Paul lays down the general principle, "to the pure [in heart] all things are pure" and this inward perspective produces outward purity as well.

Legalism always presumes everyone can and must make himself pure to be acceptable to God by following certain rituals, traditions or following ceremonies or regulations and by avoiding a list of actions that are considered sinful. This has been the basic heresy through the history, which has believed in a sacramental, sacerdotal or ritualistic religion whether Jewish, Catholic, Protestant, Orthodox, Islamic or cultic. They are basically all the same false idea of a ritualistic righteousness.

Paul describes those who promote that foundational heresy in his letter to the church at Rome, saying of them, "For not knowing about God's righteousness, and seeking to establish their own, they did not subject themselves to the righteousness of God" (Rom. 10:3).

From the beginning of time men have attempted to gain acceptance with God by lighting candles, burning incense, counting beads, repeating prescribed prayers, bowing or facing a certain direction when praying, having visions or mystical experiences, being baptized or taking the Lord's supper in order to be saved or to improve their odds of being acceptable to God.

By refusing to submit to the righteousness of God and recognize that no one could ever be comparable to His righteousness, the sinner tries in vain to be good enough for God. Only by faith and dependence in His promise to cleanse and forgive while granting to the sinner God's perfect righteousness as a free gift can unworthy man ever be saved.

To the "defiled and unbelieving nothing is pure." This is because inwardly in his heart he has refused to trust in God's truth. "For out of the heart come evil thoughts, murders, adulteries, fornications, thefts, false witness, slanders. These are the things which defile the man; but to eat with unwashed hands does not defile the man." (Matt 15:19-20).

Peter heard this but did not understand it for years. In fact, ten years later Peter did not want to partake of ceremonial unclean animals in a dream, even when God commanded him to do so; immediately thereafter, he was invited to preach to a Gentile family.

Peter finally understood God's plan: "if God gave them the same gift as he also gave us after believing in the Lord Jesus Christ, who was I to hinder God?" (Act 11:17 NET).

Once a person buys into a legalistic mind-set, he sees himself a good, more spiritual than others and more intimate with God than others; meanwhile he sees others with destain, rejection, sinful, unlovely, and needing to repent and become like him.

Reflection: What do the following verses add to this discussion?

Col 2:20-23

1 Tim 4:4-5

1:16 "They profess to know God, but in works they deny Him, being abominable, disobedient, and disqualified for every good work."

These false teachers are professing Christians, they "profess to know God;" (1:16a) in fact, they are convinced they know Him better than anyone else. "But by their deeds they deny Him" (1:16b) because they refuse to acknowledge or believe that they are vile and guilty sinners needed His forgiveness as their only hope of acceptance.

Thus they do not know Him at all. Self-righteousness prides itself in its superiority and its higher level of spirituality, but is ugly and "abominable, disobedient, and disqualified for every good work" (1:16c)

Their false piety only covers their judgmental, critical, and vindictive spirits, making them more harmful to God's people than helpful. As Jeremiah said "they [do not] furnish [God's] people the slightest benefit" (Jer. 23:32).

Remember their error: they teach that anyone can obey a set of rules and become acceptable to God. On the other hand, this is not referring to believers who want to do right or have personal convictions and seek to obey the commands in the NT. Can you see the difference?

Reflection: Do I have the symptoms of these legalists? Do I feel that I'm a pretty good person and I'll keep trying to be better?

Do I feel that my sinfulness has no recourse within me, and my only hope is in the Savior who takes care of my sin and gives me righteousness that God will accept?

CHAP

CHAPTER 2

CHARACTERISTICS OF
A HEALTHY CHURCH

"Churches should be structured
to facilitate a mentoring ministry
that engages most people in the
membership."

Titus 2
The Characteristics of a healthy church

A body of believers dedicated to communicating genuine love for each other can have a strong attraction to a world where selfishness reigns supreme. Titus 2 describes the beautiful characteristics of a healthy church that demonstrates the power to transform lives, build a generational legacy and appreciate the joy of our salvation.

Structures for applications
2:1 "But as for you, speak the things which are proper for sound doctrine:"

Paul contrasts what Titus is to teach as compared to the teachings of false teachers by commanding Titus to "be continually speaking" [the meaning of the progressive sense of the present imperative] biblical concepts, which are "proper" (lit., "be conspicuous or fit") "for sound" (*hugiaino*, "healthy") "doctrine" (i.e.,"teaching or instruction").

The word for "proper" is used in Eph 5:3 where Paul declared believers were to be different: "But fornication and all uncleanness or covetousness, let it not even be named among you, as is fitting for saints" (Eph 5:3).

Believers' lives are to "fit" or reflect what is believed about righteous living. Titus was to constantly and repeatedly emphasize spiritually healthy teachings, illustrating the life of Christ being lived out through each person.

Reflection: How would you define "unhealthy" teachings? (hint: examine the context)

1 Tim 6:3

2 Tim 1:13

Pastors are to be dedicated to equipping (Eph 4:12) and maturing the church members in *depth*, allowing God to develop the *breath* of the ministry (1 Cor 3:6;

2 Cor 9:10) that He wants. Reversing this priority engenders weaknesses in the churches.

Elder men as examples

2:2 "that the older men be sober, reverent, temperate, sound in faith, in love, in patience;"

In this context the "older men" (*presbutas*, "elder") is a different word used for the "elders" (*presbuteros*) of the church in 1:5. Paul referred to himself with this term (Philem. 9). W. Mounce states, "Hippocrates's discussion of the seven stages of life, the sixth being πρεσβύτης, which he identifies as being fifty to fifty-six years of age." (Mounce, W. D. (2000). *Pastoral Epistles*. Vol. 46. Dallas: Word, Incorporated, p. 408)

Ideally, Job described the value of the elderly: "Is not wisdom found among the aged? Does not long life bring understanding?" (Job 12:12 ᴺᴱᵀ). Life's lessons can be the "school of hard knocks," and/or personal development over time all of which need to be passed on to another generation, if they will listen.

However, being older or even having been a Christian for a long time does not guarantee maturity and exemplary living. Peter insisted that believers "make every effort to add to your faith" seven characteristics (2 Pet 1:5-7).

John Wesley's latter days are described as continuing to be productive to the end:

> At the age of 83—after having traveled some 250,000 miles on horse-back, preached more than 40,000 sermons, and produced some 200 books and pamphlets—John Wesley regretted that he was unable to read and write for more than 15 hours a day without his eyes becoming too tired to work. After his 86th birthday, he admitted to an increasing tendency to lie in bed until 5:30 in the morning! (MacArthur,1996, 72).

We cannot all be John Wesley, but we can seek to continue to have goals of growing spiritually and biblically. Paul now gives four qualities for all the older men in the church so they can become credible mentors of a younger generation:

1. "Sober" means to be "clear-minded, temperate; abstaining from wine, either entirely or at least from its immoderate use." It is used of "bishops" (1 Tim 3:2) and deacons' wives (1 Tim 3:11). It refers to avoiding extravagance, extremes and over-indulgence.
2. "Reverent" means "dignified or worthy of respect." Paul also used this word to describe deacons (1 Tim 3:8) and their wives (1 Tim 3:11). The word does not mean haughtiness or high-class attitudes, but refers to seriousness as opposed to frivolous superficiality.
3. "Temperate" means "sensible, self-controlled, curbing one's desires and impulses. " It is used also for mature women (2:4), younger women (2:5), and younger men (2:7). As a requirement for an elder/pastor (1 Tim 3:2), they are to reject worldly standards and resist carnal attractions.
4. "Sound" or "healthy" or "metaphorically, of Christians whose opinions are free from any mixture of error." It refers to characteristics that generate spiritual maturity in Christ-likeness. They avoid unhealthy extremes and extra-biblical notions however popular.

This "soundness" is especially demonstrated in their areas: faith, love and perseverance [patience].

First, elderly men are to be healthy in "faith." This means to have learned that God can be trusted in the difficulties of life without questioning His wisdom (James 1:2-8) as Jesus did in the midst of a storm (Matt 8:24-26).

Secondly, elderly men are to be healthy in "love" in every aspect, toward God, toward others and toward the unsaved. They are to demonstrate love by caring more for others than for themselves (Phil 2:2-4). They are always encouraging and doing things for others to show them the love of Christ.

Thirdly, elderly men are to be healthy in "perseverance," enduring difficulties of disappointments, disillusionments, deterioration of physical health or loneliness (1 Cor 4:12; 9:12; 13:7) as Jesus did (Heb 12:2). Like Abraham "he was looking forward to the city with firm foundations, whose architect and builder is God. (Heb 11:10 NET).

Reflection: Are you learning the lessons of wisdom for understanding and accepting life's twists and the hurts of some relationships to enable you to "have fought the good fight, to have finished the race, to have kept the faith" (2 Tim

4:7)?

What principle(s) would you share from your experiences with your grandchildren about how to honor Christ in all life's circumstances?

Elder women as examples and mentors in seven areas

2:3 "the older women likewise, that they be reverent in behavior, not slanderers, not given to much wine, teachers of good things—"

The phrase "older women" (*presbytidas*), likewise is a different word from the feminine form of the word for "elders" (*presbuteros*) in 1:5, which probably refers to the age of women whose children are raised and have established their own homes.

A woman's responsibilities change at this stage of life to become a mentor of other women and more focused lover of her husband. This new focus enables victory over "feelings of uselessness, loneliness, low self-esteem, and self-pity."

"A woman's childbearing ends around 40-45 years of age, and child rearing ends around 50-60 years of age. It is likely 'older women,' therefore, refers to women around 60 years of age," the same age that Paul used to describe the widowed woman who "trusts in God and continues in supplications and prayers night and day. ... Do not let a widow under sixty years old be taken into the number, ... [she must be] well reported for good works: if she has brought up children, if she has lodged strangers, if she has washed the saints' feet, if she has relieved the afflicted, if she has diligently followed every good work." (1Tim 5:5, 9, 10). Married or widowed older women can have a strategic ministry.

Reflection: How many ministries can you think of that senior women can have an effective role in fulfilling?

Luke 2:37

Luke 2:38

Churches should be structured to facilitate a mentoring ministry that engages most people in the membership. Paul challenges that the senior women in a church dedicate themselves to five self-development goals and a curriculum of seven learning objectives for mentoring young wives that will enrich and build the credibility of the overall church ministry.

(1) "Be reverent in behavior,"

The word used for "reverent" means to be "suitable to what is sacred" (lit., "temple" + "to be fitting"), thus "a person who honors God in his conduct." They are to dress in a Christ-honoring manner as described in 1 Tim 2:9-11. "The simple meaning is that we must take seriously the fact that we belong to God" (TDNT 3:254) and show it.

(2) "Not slanderers,"
The word used is *diabolos*, "a false accuser, malicious gossips" a term used as a title for the devil thirty-four times, who is the "accuser of the brethren before God (Rev 12:9, 10; Job 1-2). By judging others or destroying the reputation of any believer is playing into the hands of the devil in his attempt to ruin the lives of Christians.

Reflection: Review all the conversations you have had or listened to over the past few days. When other people were referred to, was it in a positive and constructive tone, or a negative, demeaning and defaming tenor? What should you have done when this kind of conversation began?

(3) "Not given to much wine,"
The word "given to" translates *douloo*, "to enslave;" from which we get the word *doulos*, "slave." It means literally "to be held and controlled against one's will." Alcoholism must have been a major problem in the first century since it was an issue for every church leader in every list (1 Tim 3:3, 8; Titus 1:7; and 1 Tim 5:23). But the problem was even more exaggerated in Crete.

When an elderly person becomes addicted to "much wine" Christ's name is dishonored, the reputation of the church is disgraced and her example of drinking alcohol can tempt others to drink too much.

41

Reflection: How does 1 Cor 14:21 apply in this area of life? Are you willing to abstain from drinking alcoholic drinks for the ministry? How do you define "addiction?"

(4) "Teachers of good things"
In the original this phrase is one word (*kalodidaskalos*) and it only occurs here in Greek literature, so it may have been created by Paul, or the Lord. This "teacher" is not an official position in the church, but speaks of one who counsels and mentors other women.

"The older women should be those who are "teaching what is good"—not in the sense of 1 Tim. 2:12, which is forbidden to women, but as is indicated by what follows, teaching younger women about their duties." (Knight, 1992, 307).

God's plan of older women are mentoring younger women as a key to building up solid families among the believers.

Reflections: Were you ever mentored by a mature Christian woman (or by a man if you are a man)?

What do you wish you could have learned if you had you had a good mentor? This answer may be your focus for a ministry to others.

(5) Teachers of younger wives:
2:4a "that they admonish the young women…"

The original structure of this verse begins with a *hina* clause, which introduces a purpose clause ("in order that…"); however, the purpose seems to be post-poned until the end of verse 5, "that the word of God may not be blasphemed" ["dishonored"NAS, or "discredited"NET].

The first lesson for young wives is to learn to "be sober," as a verb means "to be mentally stable; to bring someone to his senses." There are many enemies of mental stability in every culture due to pressures of the marriage relationship and unending, exhausting work in raising children.

It is easy to accept thoughts that lead to depressions and bitterness against their lot in life. The counsel should focus on building personal satisfaction in their relationship with Christ and to live for eternity's values and purposes. Rejection of the following values in the Christian family has destroyed families and lives in the name of feminist rights. God's Word is dishonored and defamed by accusations of being sexist, chauvinistic and too restrictive, making God's values irrelevant and non-binding for women today.

Regardless of how our culture and society's values differ from God's Word, the Christian must trust God's plan for all relationships, especially His design for women. The god of this world will always develop a culture that contradicts God's Word, yet everything God reveals about women fulfills their created purpose, and magnifies their unique design to become a blessing to everyone and find genuine fulfillment. Self-centeredness always leads to destruction and ruin.

Young wives

1. Need to be taught to love their husbands
2:4b "... the young women to love their husbands,"

This phrase ties the mature women to a mentoring relationship with the "young women." They are to "admonish" (Greek: "encourage, advise, urge") young wives to "love their husbands." This is one word in the original, *philandros*, which is similar to *philoteknos*, "loving one's children." Both are compounds with *philos*, "loving," that occur only here in the NT.

This is especially appropriate in cultures where arranged marriages are the accepted norm. This is not a romantic love in Greek (*eros*), rather a willing, committed love that seeks to meet the needs of another (husband and children) and thus finding one's greatest fulfillment in their satisfaction.

A tomb inscription of the time of the Emperor Hadrian (3rd Cent.) read, "Julius Bassus to Otacilia Polla, his sweetest wife. Loving her husband (*philandros*) and loving her children (*philoteknos*), she lived with him unblameably for 30 years."

Ironically, this self-giving love produces the deepest joy and contentment in God's design, especially when this love is appreciated and honored by the recipients (especially husbands and children). Regardless of the initial romantic feelings, the wife needs to learn how to love her husband, even if he is unloving, uncaring, unfaithful or ungrateful (1 Pet 3:1). God's grace is sufficient.

This kind of love is not natural in young women. Youth tends to be self-centered. They need the help of mature women who have learned the benefits of following God's principles in marriage. It means sacrificial giving for the benefit of others and finding joy in doing so. Jesus taught, "If you love only those who love you, what reward is there for that? Even corrupt tax collectors do that much." (Mat 5:46 ᴺᴸᵀ)

Without learning this kind of married love, women can find marriage unappealing because it interferes with their agenda. Any marriage is salvageable if God's principles are taken seriously and applied. This is how all believers are supposed to be trained to serve each other. Lessons learned in the family are then extended to the church relationships.

Reflection: How do the admonitions of Phil 2:2-4 apply to the marriage relationship? Then to other believers?

2. Need to be taught to love their children
2:4c "... to love their children,"

Like the love (*philos*) to the husband, so is the love to the children in marriage to be selfless and sacrificial. This is not optional. It is not based on the positive response of the children or their physical attractiveness, personalities, intelligence or personal benefit. Nor is it motivated by how much affection is expressed to the mother (Matt 5:46).

It is based on the child's need for a caring, training parent who seeks to show them the love of God and to teach them how to walk through life with Him and His Word.

Reflection: How would you describe the kind of lessons a young mother needs to know about child rearing?

Does contemporary psychological ideas take priority over biblical principles? Do you know where these two concepts contrast? Which do you chose?

3. Need to be taught to be sensible.
2:5a "to be discreet,"

The word "discreet" (*sophron*) means to be "of a sound mind, in one's senses; curbing one's desires and impulses; self-controlled." Maturity is learning not to follow life's impulses or feelings, but to choose to live by principles, especially the commands in the NT, regardless of one's feelings. Life is not to be reactionary, but proactive. Help is always needed here. Advice is to be sought from wiser, mature women.

4. Need to be taught to be pure
2:5b "... chaste,"

The word "chaste" (*hagnos*) means "pure, holy," especially in regard to sexual purity and marital fidelity. Often fidelity in marriage needs a mentor or someone with whom to be accountable, who can ask the tough questions. Disillusionment and selfishness leads to dissatisfaction, then the seeking of substitutes.

"Marriage must be honored among all and the marriage bed kept undefiled, for God will judge sexually immoral people and adulterers." (Heb 13:4 NET) Beware of allowing thoughts of emotional satisfaction in fantasy thinking, readings or daydreaming of a better relationship outside of marriage. Dream of how to make your marriage better. Be creative.

Reflection: If someone is not afraid that God will chasten sexually immoral acts or thoughts, how do you think this will affect one's resistance to temptation?

5. Need to be taught to be homemakers
2:5c "... homemakers,"

The word "homemaker" means "workers at home" (NAS). This may be the most difficult step for the contemporary wife: how to be fulfilled with being a homemaker wife, as opposed to being a successful businesswoman.

With modern conveniences boredom, dissatisfaction and temptations (with TV fantasies) become more common. It was estimated that in 2000, 90 percent of all women between the ages of 16 and 65 would have jobs outside the home. (MacArthur 1996, 85).

In general, the culture looks down on homemaker-wives; however, the high value of a woman's chief fulfillment comes from the family and her home. As a result there are many dysfunctional families in our churches with terrible moral consequences in our young people.

Reflection: How do these verses reinforce this principle?

1 Tim 5:14

Prov 31:10-31

6. Need to be taught to be good
2:5d "... good,"

The word means to be "benevolent, profitable, or useful," also "pleasant, agreeable, joyful, happy" especially to others. Wives need to be taught how to maintain these attitudes well, so as to be a benefit to everyone and a pleasant person to be around.

7. Need to be taught to be obedient
2:5e "... obedient to their own husbands,"

The word for "obedient" is "to place in order, to place under in an orderly fashion." This is a common instruction in Paul's writings (1 Tim 2:11; Col 3:18; Eph 5:21-23; 1 Pet 3:1, 5). The phrase "to their own..." signifies that this is not speaking of one gender to another outside of marriage, but about how the husband and wife are to relate and understand each other.

The verbal participial form means to be "continually submitting themselves … " in a voluntary submission. This submission is based on the principle that God has declared the man as the "head" or the one responsible for the marriage (Eph 5:22-24; 1 Cor 11:3). Paul does not seem to regard submission as problematic requiring explanation or qualifications.

Reason for teaching young wives
2:5f "… that the word of God may not be blasphemed."

This is the second purpose clause (introduced by the Greek word *hina*). This one and the third one in verse 10 emphasize the value of protecting the reputation of God's Word. In 1 Tim 5:14-15 a similar context leads up to the phrase, "to give the enemy no occasion for reproach, for some have already turned aside to follow Satan."

Any time God's Word is disregarded Satan uses it to denigrate or make ridiculous what God has said, thus dishonoring God Himself. To "blaspheme" is to "speak evil of" something. In Romans 2:24 Paul writes of the Jews that "God's name is blasphemed among the Gentiles because of you," and the attitude of the slaves can generate the same response (1 Tim 6:1).

Some commentators (i.e., Fee) say that this is Paul's opinion, not God's, or that this is merely a cultural compliance that is not applicable today, but to say that only this last trait is merely cultural and all the rest are applicable is poor exegesis. If all Scripture is inspired of God, He included it for a good reason.

Reflection: If unbelievers judge the truth and power of the Word of God by the way we live, then we must have a different perspective from the world. What are the potential consequences of practicing this principle of submission in 1 Pet 3:1-2?

Phil 2:15

Single young men

As with the young women, the phrase "young men" describes an age group from marriageable age up to about 60 years old.

Young men are to be serious and practical
2:6 "Likewise exhort~~ the young men to be sober-minded,"

The word "likewise" ties this phrase and obligation to the foregoing principle of an elder person mentoring as well.

The word for "continually be exhorting" (meaning of the present progressive imperative) is the word *parakaleo*, "to strongly entreat, beg, beseech." Seldom do people learn to apply God's Word with a single mention or exhortation. It takes constant repetition of truths.

The primary objective of this urging is to be "sober-minded" or "sensible," or "self-controlled," as opposed to being impulsive, passionate, ambitious, volatile or arrogant. This is the same virtue demanded of a bishop/elder/pastor (Tit 1:8; 1 Tim 3:2) and of aged men (Titus 2:2). The repeated insistence of this virtue implies that the opposite natural characteristic was common in Crete.

Reflection: How does "sober-minded" display maturity in young men?

The Example of Titus
2:7a "In all things showing yourself to be a pattern of good works;"

"In all things" probably goes with the preceding verses challenging Titus to be a man of God as a "pattern" or "model" [*tupos*, "a stamped image or impression"] of "good works," that is, all of the foregoing examples of spiritual maturity.

> It may be assumed that about the year 51, when Timothy joined Paul who was on his second missionary journey, the former had reached the age of 22–27 years of age. It is hardly probable that the apostle would have permitted a man even younger than that to join him in such a difficult task. Besides, we know that Timothy must have reached a degree

of maturity even during Paul's first missionary journey, for it was then that he had "confessed his faith." If this calculation be correct, then Timothy is now—i.e., about the year 63—somewhere between 34 and 39 years of age. According to Ireneus, the first stage of life embraces thirty years and extends onward until forty years (*Against Heresies, II.* xxii). Hence, Timothy was still "a young man." (Hendriksen, Kistemaker 1953–2001, 157).

If a person does not follow his own teaching or exhorting, he is viewed as a hypocrite, regardless of how good or biblical his teaching or counsel may be. Luther wrote on Titus 2:5, "Because the heathen cannot see our faith, they ought to see our works, then hear our doctrine, and then be converted" (J. Pelikan, ed., *Luther's Works*, (St. Louis: Concordia, 1966) 29:57).

Reflection: What do the following verses indicate about the importance of our example?

1 Tim 4:12

1 Thes 1:7

2 Thes 3:9

Phil 3:17

Example in teaching and living
2:7b "… in doctrine showing integrity, reverence, incorruptibility,"

A similar challenge was given to Timothy to be the believer's model ("in speech, in conduct, in love, in faith, in purity" – 1 Tim 4:12). This was the model of Paul: admonish the younger men (v. 6) and give them a good example to follow (vs. 7-8). Precept and example are inseparable in the ministry, and usually one's example speaks louder than his words—but ideally, reinforces them.

Reflection: Why did Paul place such an emphasis on being an example?
2 Thes 3:9

Phil 3:17

Titus' teaching had to demonstrate three characteristics (2:7b):

Integrity – Titus' faithfulness to the word and purity of motive must show that he was not infected with the distortions of the false teachers. This word only occurs here in the NT. It means "soundness, single-mindedness."
Reverence – Titus' attitude and manner must show the dignity or seriousness with which he undertakes his responsibility.
Incorruptibility—Titus' entire message must be sound and not liable to rebuke.

As a result Titus, like Paul, could exhort the believers to "be imitators of me, just as I also am of Christ" (1 Cor 11:1; 4:16; Phil 3:17).

> Members of the church at Ephesus might resist the bare words that he taught, but they could not deny the power of the truths that were faithfully exemplified in his life. If his speech in daily living, not just "from the pulpit," was godly; if the conduct of his personal life was moral and selfless; if his love for the Lord and for fellow believers was genuine; if his faith was manifested in genuine trust in the Lord; and if his life was characterized by moral purity; he could be sure that his ministry would be effective, that it would be blessed and bear fruit. (MacArthur 1996, 93).

Reflection: What are the most important characteristics that you look for in a leader, which virtually obligates you to listen to and want to follow him?

2:8a "… sound speech that cannot be condemned,"

"Sound speech" means "healthy and whole" that "cannot be condemned." Believers are to live and speak in such a manner that no charges can justifiable be brought against the message of the gospel. They are to live purposefully, demonstrating that God's will from His Word is the best way to live.

Paul is concerned about the testimony of the young men before a critical world. James put it this way, "If you claim to be religious but don't control your tongue, you are fooling yourself, and your religion is worthless. (Jam 1:26 NLT).

This does not mean that no one will contradict or judge you, but that there will be no justification for an accusation of hypocrisy or deviant concepts different from Paul (2 Tim 1:13) or from Jesus' teachings (1 Tim 6:3).

Reflection: What do these verses tell us about "sound speech?"

Eph 4:29

Eph 6:19

The Purpose
2:8b "… that one who is an opponent may be ashamed, having nothing evil to say of you."

The godly lives of the church members and its leader(s) are to put to shame the critics of the church, that is, they would be embarrassed to make false accusations.

The Jewish critics who thought they were so righteous and that the Gentiles were unworthy of the gospel, now would see that Gentiles genuinely converted are as godly as any faithful Jewish believer. They would see the proof that God's word and the power of Christ to redeem and transform sinners is as effective among all Gentiles as Jewish Christians.

For non-believers to observe misconduct or inconsistencies of any Christian and especially of a leader in the church, will have negative consequences for the entire Christian community and the impact of the gospel message. People tend to listen to someone they trust.

Reflections: In the following verses what is the key element to the effectiveness of the gospel proclamation?

1 Pet 2:11-12

Matt 5:16

Servants/Employees

2:9a "Exhort bondservants to be obedient to their own masters..."

The fifth category of believers is not based on age but social standing. Slaves comprised the majority of the population of the Roman Empire. Many of them were poorly treated, but Paul never mentions this social injustice. He teaches how to live for Christ in the midst of any unfair economic/political system.

Some will serve and others will be served. God's word does not seek to change social structures, but rather our thinking about relationships as we seek to bring honor to Christ everywhere and in every situation.
The most fertile field for evangelism is where Christians work. Unbelievers can observe our attitudes in a multitude of situations and will judge whether we are genuinely transformed by the gospel or merely faking it.

Does the believer demonstrate patience or impatience, kindness or disinterest, selflessness or selfishness, honesty or dishonesty, clean speech or vulgar language, clean jokes or dirty jokes? Observers of Christians will listen to those having a marked difference in attitude and efforts especially at work. Paul now gives six characteristics of a faithful believing slave/employee.

1) Submissive:
2:9a "...be obedient to their own masters..."

The believing slave is to be subject to his master and treat him "worthy of all respect" (1 Tim 6:1). This submission is essential to a family where the children are to be subject to their parents (Eph 6:1; Col 3:20). The same submission is vital in governments where people are to be submissive to their leaders (Rom 13:1-7; Tit 3:1). The submission of a slave/employee is addressed to other Christians as well (Eph 5:21; 1 Cor 16:16/ Rom 13:1; 1 Pet 2:13; Eph 5:22; Col 3:18; 1 Pet 3:1, 5)

It is an essential in the workplace where rebellion and strikes dishonor God. The "masters" translates the word *despotes*, someone with absolute author- ity. These same principles apply to employees today even if the employer is unreasonable and abusive (1 Pet 2:18-10). Verse 10 implies that this is especially important with unsaved masters/employers. Some situations may require more grace than others, but the objective is to be a living testimony of

His transforming power.

2) Excellence
2:9b "… to be well pleasing in all things,"

The word "well-pleasing" is generally used for pleasing God (Rom 12:1-2; 2 Cor 5:9; Phil 4:18; Eph 5:10). Being well-pleasing to our heavenly Master includes doing excellent tasks for our earthly master or employer.

If a slave had a Christian master they should not think that they could serve less because we "are all one in Christ Jesus" (Gal 3:28). The truth is that equality in the spiritual realm is not transferred to equality in the social or earthly realm. "Those who are under the yoke as slaves must regard their own masters as deserving of full respect. This will prevent the name of God and Christian teaching from being discredited. But those who have believing masters must not show them less respect because they are brothers. Instead they are to serve all the more, because those who benefit from their service are believers and dearly loved. Teach them and exhort them about these things. (1 Tim 6:1-2 NET).

The biblical attitude is passively be submissive and to fulfill expectations by working hard and doing excellent work so the company can grow and increase in income, thus being enabled them to hire more people with whom to share the gospel. The motive of believers is always to enhance the reputation of Christ through their excellence.

3) Respectful
2:9c "…not answering back,"

The Christian worker is always respectful to his superior, especially by "not answering back" means to "speak against, contradict, or decline to obey or declare one's self against him." Here the reference means to oppose or slander your authorities behind their backs. The word conveys the idea of active disobedience, resistance, rebellion and strife.

Reflection: What does Col 3:22 add to this picture of a slave/employee's testimony?

4) Honesty
2:10a "not pilfering"

"Pilfering" originally means "to put aside for oneself or misappropriate" and became the word for stealing by embezzlement. The use of the verb in Acts 5:2,3 describes how Ananias and Sapphira "held back" or "withdrew" a portion of what had been promised to the church, while pretending to have given all of the proceeds from the sale of their property and, therefore, it technically belonged to someone else.
Slaves would have access to many things. They might rationalize that the owner would never miss something or he deserved better than he was receiving so he could take a little something and feel justified in doing it.

There are many ways of doing this today: putting extra time on time-sheets, expense reports, using office supplies for personal projects, unauthorized phone calls, or using company vehicles for personal use, etc.. Sooner or later your superiors become aware or suspicious of what is happening. Anything you say thereafter is suspect of deceit or discredited as being false.

Unbelievers look for anything illegitimate to disregard the gospel message or refuse an invitation to church.

5) Loyalty
2:10b "… but showing all good fidelity,

The word for "fidelity," *pistos*, is the word for "faith" or "faithfulness," depending on the context. Here the idea is that the believing slave is to be unquestionably trustworthy and reliable, even when no one is watching. Building this reputation for his owner becomes the platform for believing anything the slave may say.

6) Over all motivation
2:10c "… that they may adorn the doctrine of God our Savior in all things."

Here is another purpose statement (introduced by Gk., *hina*) that gives the reason for the aforementioned behavior: the Christian slave/employer is to honor and build up the reputation of the Lord he serves. His life and service is to "adorn the doctrine of God," that is, to make it look attractive.

The word "adorn" is *kosmeo*, from which we get the word cosmetics, the elements that women use to make themselves appear even more beautiful.

Paul was referring to the lifestyle of slaves making God appear more attractive especially by these characteristics mentioned. It is the message of salvation ("God our Savior") that needs validation by lives that are genuinely transformed by His presence within them.

The beauty of the gospel is not the logic or amazing promises, but it is the transformed lives, which reflect the beauty of the Savior who indwells the believer.

Reflection: Of these four areas of testimony of an employee, which is the most difficult to maintain or establish where you work? How can we help each other?

Doctrinal foundation of a transformed life

2:11a "For the grace of God that brings salvation has appeared to all men,"

Since the verse begins with "for" it gives the theological basis for the preceding exhortations. The "grace of God" is more than a passive divine attribute, but an active motivation for the intervention of God into the affairs of undeserving men and women to bring about His gracious purpose for their salvation.

The description of the "grace of God" is as though it were a person who "appeared to all men," in the sense that the God-man came to earth appearing in tangible form.

The word "grace" refers to a willingness to grant special favor to those who do not deserve it. God's grace was manifested in the person of Jesus Christ who was God incarnate with the purpose of taking on the full wrath of God the Father for the sins of all mankind.

Paul wrote to Timothy, "not according to our works, but according to His own purpose and grace which was granted us in Christ Jesus from all eternity, but now has been revealed by the appearing of our Savior Christ Jesus, who abolished death, and brought life and immortality to light through the gospel" (2 Tim. 1:9–10).

His "appearance" (*epiphaino*), from which we get the word epiphany, means "coming to the light." In Jesus Christ "the Word became flesh, and dwelt among us, and we beheld His glory, glory as of the only begotten from the Father, full of grace and truth .... For of His fullness we have all received, and grace upon grace" (John 1:14, 16).

His appearing was designed to save men from the corruption, deceit, destruction and damnation of sin that separates sinners from a holy God, destroying lives like a cancer. Only this cancer has a cure. It is the redemptive act of unmerited grace. In Titus 2:11-14 Paul gives four aspects or realities of God's redemptive grace:

1. Salvation from the penalty of sin (v. 11b)
2. Salvation from the power of sin (v. 12)
3. Salvation from the presence of sin (v. 13)
4. Salvation from the possession of sin (v. 14)

1. Salvation from the penalty of sin
2:11b "... that brings salvation has appeared to all men,"

"Salvation" refers to "deliverance," especially from sin and its consequences (spiritual death and separation from God), unless the context demands another concept of deliverance. "The wages of sin [always] is death" (Rom. 6:23).

Jesus scathingly warned, "You shall die in your sins; for unless you believe that I am He, you shall die in your sins" (John 8:24). To die in one's sins is to face the horrible consequence of eternal separation from God in hell.

The period of grace is only offered during this life. Not to avail oneself of His grace now is to lose it forever. Jesus warned us to be afraid that what God said, He will do: "but rather fear Him who is able to destroy both soul and body in hell" (Matt. 10:28).

On the other hand, Jesus declared His purpose in coming to earth saying, "I give eternal life to them, and they shall never perish; and no one shall snatch them out of My hand" (10:28). Only the believer has reason to never fear hell, because they trust the promise of Christ.

This amazing offer of a fully paid salvation has only occurred once on earth when Christ became the "Savior of all men, especially of believers" (1 Tim 4:10). The verb "has appeared" is the aorist tense which means a one-time appearing.

The offer is universal, but the application is only for those who believe and receive the offer. God "desires all men to be saved and to come to the knowledge of the truth" (1 Tim. 2:4), but He does not force anyone to believe in Him. As an infinite Being, His death for man's sins was likewise infinite in its payment offer, but only applicable to those who see themselves as sinful people who are desperate for relief from their guilt and just condemnation. The only offer in the world for man's dilemma is the death of Christ for the "wages of [my] sins" (Rom 6:23).

To ignore it now, is to lose it forever. The moment one dies, the offer ends: "And as it is appointed for men to die once, but after this the judgment, (Heb 9:27). Woe to the person who ignores God's gracious offer.

Reflection: Do you know how to explain God's salvation to an unbeliever? Practice it with a friend.

2. Salvation from the power of sin
2:12 "teaching us that, denying ungodliness and worldly lusts, we should live soberly, righteously, and godly in the present age,"

"Teaching" is the word *paideuo* from which we get the word pedagogy. The subject of this action is "the grace of God," which is personified in the person of Jesus Christ, the incarnate Grace of God. He came not only as a Savior, but also as a Teacher.

Paul told the Corinthians, "Now we have received, not the spirit of the world, but the Spirit who is from God, that we might know the things freely given to us by God, which things we also speak, not in words taught by human wisdom, but in those taught by the Spirit, combining spiritual thoughts with spiritual words" (1 Cor. 2:12–13).

To come to Christ in salvation one must recognize the horrible state we are in before our God due to the offensiveness and wickedness of our personal sins. It is not just a free ticket to heaven we seek, but a full and painful payment for our sins. In spite The agony of the Cross and the crushing separation from the Father (Matt 27:46) He willingly paid for our indulgence in sinful practices. After this realization how could we want to enjoy returning to such sins that only inflicted more wrath from the Father?

Now we see life differently. "Just as you presented your members as slaves to impurity and to lawlessness, resulting in further lawlessness," Paul explained to believers in Rome, "so now present your members as slaves to righteousness, resulting in sanctification" (Rom. 6:19).

First we are to be "denying ungodliness," or the lack of respect or fear of God. The true believer cannot sin without a sense of guilt. It is "against all ungodliness and unrighteousness of men" that "the wrath of God is revealed from heaven" (Rom. 1:18). Believers see sin differently than unbelievers.

After giving a long list of "the deeds of the flesh: immorality, impurity, sensuality, idolatry, sorcery, enmities, strife, jealousy, outbursts of anger, disputes, dissensions, factions, envying, drunkenness, carousing, and things like these," Paul declares "that those who practice such things shall not inherit the kingdom of God …Those who belong to Christ Jesus have crucified the flesh with its passions and desires" (Gal. 5:19–21, 24).

Secondly, we are to deny "world lusts," referring to sins that we might not have physically committed, but we still wanted or dreamed of doing. These include numerous kinds of lusts, cravings, ambitions or virtual practices. These are destructive, though internal, passions: as Paul wrote, "foolish and harmful desires, which plunge men into ruin and destruction" (1 Tim. 6:9).

The primary solution is to "walk by the Spirit, [so we] will not carry out" the worldly desires "of the flesh" (Gal. 5:16).

Thirdly, on the contrary, we are to "live soberly, righteousness and godly in this present age." Since God declared us righteous (because He gave us His righteousness – 1 Cor 5:21) now we are to actively live out that inward passive righteousness.

The characteristic of "soberly" is the same word that has appeared four times in Titus as the quality of an elder (1:8), older mature men (2:2), mature women (2:5) and young men (2:6). A sober or sensible person is progressively gaining control over his former fleshly or carnal way of life.

Fourthly, the grace of God teaches us how to live "righteously," that is faithfully obeying the instructions and commands of God's Word. Now God's way of seeing life becomes our way of understanding life. His commands become our guide and lamp to our feet. "Therefore I love Your commandments More than gold, yes, than fine gold! (Psa 119:127).

Jesus said, "If you love me, you will obey my commandments." (John 14:15 NET). This does not mean merely staying out of trouble, but consciously deciding to practice all the commands of the NT (Matt 28:20).

Reflection: Which of these four is the most difficult? Are you willing to be accountable to someone for growing in this area so your new life becomes more evident?

3. Salvation from the presence of sin
2:13 "looking for the blessed hope and glorious appearing of our great God and Savior Jesus Christ,"

Someday Jesus is coming again to take us into His presence forever. If we are alive at that moment in time (1 Cor 15:51-53), we will never die physically, but will be transformed in a second into our glorified bodies and taken away to be with Him. The word "looking for" has the notion of "longing and waiting for something" and of an eager expectation.

The Rapture (described in 1 Thes 4:15-17) is the event when all believers are transformed into glorified bodies and ascend into the clouds to meet the Lord, while back on earth a series of horrific events begins, which are described in

Revelation 4-19 to occur in seven years.

At the end of the seven years of tribulation Christ returns to earth (not just in the clouds) at His Second Coming to set up His kingdom. Christ will be seen in His blinding Shekinah glory that Peter, James and John witnessed on the Mount of Transfiguration (Matt 17:1-8).

"Our great God and Savior Jesus Christ" is one of a number of clear declarations of the deity of Christ (John 1:1-18; Rom 9:5; Heb 1:1-3). These titles cannot refer to separate Persons of the Godhead, but rather grammatically are a clear affirmation of the Christ's deity.

First, there is only one article before "*the* God and Savior." If they were separate beings the Greek grammar would need to say, "the God and the Savior."

Secondly, the singular pronouns "who" and "Himself" refer back to a single person, not two persons.

Thirdly, the NT only speaks of the "appearing" or Second Coming of the Son, and nowhere refers to the coming of God the Father.

Reflection: Can you explain how much you want to be alive at the Rapture of the church? What is so "glorious" about it?

4. Salvation from sin's possession
2:14 "who gave Himself for us, that He might redeem us from every lawless deed and purify for Himself His own special people, zealous for good works."

The unsaved are enslaved to sin to one degree or another. In the Book of Romans Paul asked, "Do you not know that when you present yourselves to someone as slaves for obedience, you are slaves of the one whom you obey, either of sin resulting in death, or of obedience resulting in righteousness?" (Rom. 6:16).

Earlier Paul had stated, "knowing this, that our old self was crucified with Him, that our body of sin might be done away with, that we should no longer be slaves to sin; for he who has died is freed from sin" (6:5–7). We have been set free and empowered to remain free from the dominion of sin.

Our Savior "gave Himself for us that He might redeem us from every lawless deed..." All three verbs, "gave Himself," "might redeem us," and "purify for Himself," are all aorist verbs describing a once and for all event of a completed action).

"Redeem" means to be released from being held captive as a prisoner or a slave, upon receipt of a ransom payment. Peter reminded his readers, "You were not redeemed with perishable things like silver or gold from your futile way of life inherited from your forefathers, but with precious blood, as of a lamb unblemished and spotless, the blood of Christ"(1 Pet. 1:18–19).

Jesus came to earth to "give His life a ransom for many" (Mark 10:45). He "gave Himself for our sins, that He might deliver us out of this present evil age, according to the will of our God and Father" (Gal. 1:4).

Negatively, we are redeemed "from every lawless deed," that is, as Peter says, from the "fleshly lusts, which war against the soul" (1 Pet 2:11).

Reflection: Do you still have a "sin which so easily ensnares" you (Heb 12:1) that you know you need to "lay aside"? Will you ask a brother/sister in Christ to help you?

Positively, He redeemed us to "purify for Himself a people for His own possession." "Christ also loved the church and gave Himself up for her; that He might sanctify her, having cleansed her by the washing of water with the word" (Eph. 5:25–26).

The Lord's people "are a chosen race, a royal priesthood, a holy nation, a people for God's own possession, that we may proclaim the excellences of Him who has called us out of darkness into His marvelous light" (1 Pet. 2:9). His calling to Himself is always for a purpose. He has a plan for every child of His.

This amazing display of grace and powerful transformation has a purpose: His redeemed people freed from sin's death grip are now "zealous for good deeds." God's working in our lives is always for a practical purpose now.

Paul wrote, "we are [God's] workmanship, created in Christ Jesus for good works, which God prepared beforehand, that we should walk in them" (Eph. 2:10).

He creates in us the desire to do His will, then He makes us capable to accomplish whatever He puts in our hearts: For God is working in you, giving you the desire and the power to do what pleases him. (Phi 2:13 NLT). The life of the believer is an amazing adventure.

Reflection: If you knew you would be successful at any task on your heart, what would you want to do for Christ and His kingdom now?

Your desire for this goal may indicate that God has made you for this purpose.

The authority of the teacher/preacher

Authority can be intrinsic or extrinsic. Intrinsic authority is personality and respect driven, but extrinsic authority comes from outside a person, either an institution or a written contract. Our authority is primarily to stem from the apostolic authority in the revelation of God's word that we are to learn, obey and proclaim as it was intended.

The authority of the Early Church is seen in the early house churches, "They were devoting themselves to the apostles' teaching" (Act 2:42 NET). Timothy was told to "preach the word" (2 Tim 4:2), not his ideas or dreams. Peter said, "Whoever speaks, let it be with God's words." (1Pet 4:11 NET). Thus Paul commands Titus to "speak these things" because they are God's words.

The New Testament is not someone's opinions that can be discarded when controversial, but must be treated and proclaimed as though God were saying the same thing today. Paul wrote to the Corinthians to accept His writings at that level of authority: "If anyone thinks himself to be a prophet or spiritual, let him acknowledge that the things which I write to you are the commandments of the Lord. (1Cor 14:37).

Great care must be taken to assure that each verse or passage is carefully understood so that what is declared is in fact what God was saying when He inspired the original text. Our authority is this assurance.

Paul challenged future leaders to limit their teaching to the NT revelations when he wrote, "According to the grace of God given to me, like a skilled master-builder I laid a foundation, but someone else builds on it. And each one must be careful how he builds. For no one can lay any foundation other than what is being laid, which is Jesus Christ. (1Cor 3:10-11 NET).

Evangelists, pastors and teachers build up the church of the future on the foundational truths and revelations that the Apostles and prophets gave us in the NT. Biblical truths do not originate with teachers and preachers. Our authority is our conformity to the apostolic NT revelations. Going beyond this NT revelation or attempt to modify it is to exceed our given authority.

Reflection: If the church is built up by the learning and application of the revealed Word of God, then what is the chief responsibility of the pastor/elder?

Concluding commission
2:15a "Speak these things, exhort, and rebuke with all authority... "

All the verbs in 2:15 are present tense imperatives meaning to continuously or habitually practice all three actions: speaking, exhorting, and rebuking. The final negative present imperative "Let no one despise you," literally means, "Stop letting anyone despise you."

We are to "be speaking" God's word, "exhorting" to follow God's word, and "rebuking" any disobedience to God's word. As Peter wrote, we are to "speak according to the oracles of God," that is what He has already revealed in the Word of God.

Positively the church is built up when we "exhort" the believers to "obey all things that [Jesus has] commanded" (Matt 28:20). Negatively, the church needs to be "rebuked" or corrected from being disobedient or whenever a clear teaching in the NT has been violated. This takes courage and confidence that one is declaring the intent of God's Word.

Reflection: How and when would you see each of these commands being fulfilled in a church or small group?

2:15b "Let no one despise you."
Speaking with authority can provoke reactions from people that do not want
to conform to God's word. The authority is implicit in the message because
it is God's message to mankind, not Paul's or ours. "Despise" translates
periphroneo, a word that literally means "think around something, usually for
the purpose of evasion." Usually it expresses a sense of strong disagreement
or disregard. Strong's definition is: "exalt one's self in thought above a person,"
thus resulting in "disregard, look down on, despise" (BAGD).

Titus has to stop letting anyone disregard the message by disregarding him.
God's messengers cannot yield to intimidation and threats. In fact, Titus is
expected to "reprove" or "rebuke" anyone who seeks to manipulate him. God's
truth is to be proclaimed with authority, and submission to its precepts is
demanded in the church.

Though this command is written to Titus, it simultaneously supports him in his
responsibility to the churches as this letter was read to the churches in Crete.
In the same manner if this letter is studied today it will have the same impact of
protecting the pastor and yielding authority to God's Word as it is taught.

Reflection: Are you willing to handle controversial issues with a clear teaching
of God's word? Usually, those who avoid controversies are manipulating God's
word or dealing with it only superficially.

MENTORING FOR SPIRITUAL GROWTH

CHAP

TER3

LIFE IN A SECULAR SOCIETY

"Regardless of how deserving or hostile our government or neighbors may be, we are to bless the people in our lives."

Titus 3
Life in a secular society

In Paul's day the government was notorious for murderous tyrants, gross injustices, and sexual promiscuity. Perversions and prostitution, idolatry, corruption, high taxes and unfairness abounded. But neither Jesus nor Paul challenged believers to try to reform this immorality, to resist unjust laws or inhuman punishments. The NT calls believers to witness, and teach the gospel and NT principles, which open the door to the transforming power of salvation through Jesus Christ.

On the one hand, our contemporary relativistic, pluralistic society resists any outside control or restrictions, especially from the Bible. While on the other hand whatever the government declares to be legal is accepted as morally okay (i.e. abortion or gay rights). Either extreme leads to conflicts with biblical priorities. Believers learn how to navigate between these extremes and become respon- sible citizens in all spheres of their lives.

Our true citizenship belongs in heaven with the Lord according to Phil 3:20, "For our citizenship is in heaven, from which we also eagerly wait for the Savior, the Lord Jesus Christ." As Christians, we "are a chosen race, a royal priesthood, a holy nation, a people for God's own possession, that [we] may proclaim the excellences of Him who has called [us] out of darkness into His marvelous light" (1 Pet. 2:9). This is our priority.

It is for that reason our "behavior [must be] excellent among the Gentiles, so that in the thing in which they slander [us] as evildoers, they may on account of [our] good deeds, as they observe them, glorify God in the day of visitation" (1 Pet 2:12).

In the first eight verses of Titus 3 Paul wants Titus to reiterate the principles taught earlier. There are four areas to be remembering constantly:

1) Our seven duties as Christians (3:1-2)
2) Our former condition of unbelief and sin (3:3)
3) Our salvation through Jesus Christ (3:4-7)

4) Our mission to an unbelieving world (3:8)

(1) Remind them of our seven Christian duties (3:1-3)

3:1-2 "Remind~~ them to be subject to rulers and authorities, to obey, to be ready for every good work, to speak evil of no one, to be peaceable, gentle, showing all humility to all men."

After selecting and training new leaders Titus was to show them how to boldly speak, to exhort and rebuke when necessary (2:15). As part of the establishing of the church Titus was to "continually be reminding" all believers of their responsibilities.

The ministry of reminding believers of biblical principles was a core part of life transforming disciple-making. The word *hupomimnesko* means "to cause one to remember" and, in the present tense, means to continually be recalling to their conscious minds the commands of Jesus through Paul to the church. Look at these verses for the ministry of reminding each other:

"For this reason I have sent Timothy to you, who is my beloved and faithful son in the Lord, who will remind you of my ways in Christ" (1 Cor 4:17)

"For this reason I will not be negligent to remind you always of these things, though you know and are established in the present truth" (2 Pet 1:12)

Reflection: Who do you have in your life that keeps reminding you or challenging you toward more obedience to the commands, to faithfulness in prayer, Bible study, witnessing, etc.? We need each other, not just to feel good, but to grow spiritually.

Seven parts of an effective Christian Testimony:

(1) To be subject to leaders
3:1 "... be subject to rulers and authorities ..."

First, They were to be "subject" ("place in submission") to the secular government wherever they went. When enemies attempted to trap Jesus into saying something against the unjust, pagan government in His day, He responded, "render to Caesar the things that are Caesar's; and to God the things that are God's" (Matt 22:15-21). Even Jesus paid taxes (Matt 17:24-27).

Romans 13:1-7 gives seven reasons why all believers are under divine obligation to respect and obey human governments.

(1) "The governing authorities …, which exist are established by God" (v. 1).

(2) Anyone "who resists authority has opposed the ordinance of God" (v. 2a).

(3) Those who oppose such authority "will receive condemnation upon themselves" (v. 2b).

(4) Government is supposed to restrain evil and is therefore "not a cause of fear for good behavior, but for evil" (v. 3).

(5) It is divinely designed to promote the good of individuals and of society, "a minister of God to you for good" (v. 4a).

(6) Government is also divinely empowered to punish wrongdoers, if necessary, by capital punishment ("the sword"), as "an avenger who brings wrath upon the one who practices evil" (v. 4b).

(7) For believers "it is necessary to be in subjection [to government] not only because of wrath, but also for conscience' sake" (v. 5). "For because of this you also pay taxes for rulers are servants of God, devoting themselves to this very thing. Render to all what is due them: tax to whom tax is due; custom to whom custom; fear to whom fear; honor to whom honor" (vv. 6–7).

(2) To be obedient to human institutions
3:1c "… to obey"

The only exception to the command to be obedient is if a believer is commanded to do something against the commands of God. When the Sanhedrin Jewish High Council in Jerusalem commanded Peter and John ""not to speak or teach at all in the name of Jesus," the apostles replied, "Whether it is right in the sight of God to give heed to you rather than to God, you be the judge; for we cannot stop speaking what we have seen and heard" (Acts 4:18–20; cf.

5:29, 40–42).

Reflection: How can we be subject and obedient to our government and not support or oppose its corruption? How did Jesus do it?

(3) To be ready for good deeds

3:1d "… to be ready for every good work"

We need to be reminded to continually be looking for how to contribute to communities and society in general as the opportunity arises. Regardless of how deserving or hostile our government or our neighbors may be, we are to bless the people in our lives. "While we have opportunity, [we are to] do good to all men, and especially to those who are of the household of the faith" (Gal. 6:10).

Christians are to be renown for this service to society. This is not just a duty, but also an act of loving people as Jesus does and, therefore, in His place to demonstrate His care for them.

Paul had just made a stark contrast between believers and false teachers who "profess to know God, but by their deeds they deny Him, being detestable and disobedient, and worthless for any good deed" (Titus 1:16). Genuine spiritual transformation makes a practical difference.

Reflection: In our world, what kind of "good deeds" could we "be ready" to contribute to our society or government? We have to think about it and talk about it to be proactive in doing something constructive.

(4) To defame no one

3:2a "… to speak evil of no one "

The word for "speak evil" is *blasphemeo*, where we get the word blasphemy. It means "to speak reproachfully, rail at, revile" or "to slander, curse, or treat with contempt."

Even when condemning sinful acts, we must make a distinction not to malign the persons who commit such acts. It is not that we ignore things that need correcting, but that we do not say the worst about individuals habitually. How can we honestly pray for someone we just defamed? There is something more at stake:

"I urge that entreaties and prayers, petitions and thanksgivings, be made on behalf of all men," Paul admonishes, "for kings and all who are in authority, in order that we may lead a tranquil and quiet life in all godliness and dignity. This is good and acceptable in the sight of God our Savior, who desires all men to be saved and to come to the knowledge of the truth" (1 Tim. 2:1–4).

Reflection: Is gossip and "speaking evil" of someone a form of "getting even" with them? How does Romans 12: 14 and 17 apply in this context?

(5) To not be contentious
3:2b "... to be peaceable"

The word "peaceable" is a composite word (a- "not," and –machos, "battle") means "not contentious or disposed to fight," thus the idea of being friendly and peaceable toward the lost rather than quarrelsome or condemning. We should not be surprised when unbelievers behave like unbelievers.

Paul wrote to the Romans, "If possible, so far as it depends on you, live peaceably with all people." (Rom 12:18 NET). If God can unconditionally love the world and patiently does everything possible to win them to His care, surely we can follow His example, and not be hardened or indifferent toward those who do not know Him yet.

(6) To be gentle or humble
3:2c "... gentle"

The word originally meant "not insisting on every right of the letter of the law or custom, yielding, kind, courteous, tolerant" (BDAG). Paul wrote, "Let everyone see your gentleness" (Phi 4:5 NET), that is, the "branding" or reputation of Christianity is that everyone who follows Christ would be labeled as "gentle."

Church leaders are to be known for this quality of life (1 Tim 3:3); servants are to demonstrate this attribute (1 Pet 2:18) and this quality is one of the characteristics of "wisdom that is from above" (James 3:17).

Reflection: What was the appeal of Paul's argument for the Corinthians to be obedient in 2 Cor 10:1?

(7) To demonstrate care for others
3:2d "…showing all humility to all men."

This final responsibility toward the unsaved is to be "continually showing all humility to all men." The present tense again focuses on a habitual, continuous action. The idea is to be demonstrating or proving "whether by argument or by acts" (STRONG) an attitude of "humility" (*praotes*, "mildness, courtesy, considerateness, meekness," BAGD), which is a "fruit of the Spirit" (Gal 5:23) and one of the beatitudes (Matt 5:5, "Blessed are the meek…").

Paul admonishes "those who have been chosen of God, holy and beloved, [to] put on a heart of compassion, kindness, humility, gentleness [*prautēs*] and patience" (Col. 3:12[NAS]).

As with "gentleness" this word "humility" (often translated interchangeably) is a key to our effectiveness as a witness to "all men," especially those outside of Christ.

The lost are generally not interested in another religion, but in something that will make a difference in their lives, that will bring about better relationships and a sense of peace and satisfaction in this life. If the Christian is not different (especially in these seven areas) then his/her impact is only superficial.

Reflection: Explain how humility, gentleness, and care for others can have an impact for Christ on the lives of the unsaved?

(2) Remind them how we were once lost

The next five verses will deal with the theological basis for living among non-Christians and how to be effective in doing so. Paul is acknowledging that living among unbelievers is not easy, especially to be caring when they can be "hateful." Our model to follow is "the kindness and the love of God our Savior toward man" (v. 4).

Paul's argument is to show others the attitude God demonstrated to them when they were like the non-Christians are now.

3:3 "For we ourselves were also once foolish, disobedient, deceived, serving various lusts and pleasures, living in malice and envy, hateful and hating one another."

"For" introduces the reason for the previous commands. Reflection on our own former condition will motivate us to be patient, kind and gentle towards those who have not yet come to Christ. Paul on a number of occasions lists the sins of unbelievers (Rom 1:18, 21, 28-32) also in (1 Cor 6:9-11; Gal 5:19-2; Eph 4:17-19), and gives his own testimony as "formerly a blasphemer and a persecutor and a violent aggressor" (1 Tim 1:13). To a greater or lesser degree each of these seven descriptions is our testimony before coming to Christ.

First, we also were "once foolish" (*anoetos*, is a compound word: *a-* "not," plus "*-noetos* "understanding"), refers to the total ignorance of a particular area of knowledge, especially the gospel. Foolishness is living or acting on ignorance of truth or reality.

Second, we were once "disobedient" (*apeithes*) or "uncompliant," having disobeyed God's commands, whether we were aware of it or not. It does not matter "how" disobedient we were (and we do not need to make it worse than it was to be more dramatic), because guilt of any disobedience merits a full condemnation.

James explains the consequence of disobedience when he wrote, "For the one who obeys the whole law but fails in one point has become guilty of all of it." (Jam 2:10 NET). One sin of disobedience to God resulted in Adam being put out of God's presence (Gen 3).

The characteristic of disobedience begins early as Paul describe the unsaved generation as "disobedience to parents" (Rom 1:30; 2 Tim 3:2).

Third, we were once "deceived" (*planao*, "lead astray, led into error") in the passive voice, thus "being deceived" or "led astray." Satan is declared to be the one "who deceives the whole world" (Rev 12:9) and "is a liar, and the father of lies" (John 8:44). He is able to inject false ideas into the minds of men to deceive them into believing a lie (2 Thes 2:10-11).

Paul warned Timothy of Satan's ability to deceive when he wrote, "Now the Spirit explicitly says that in the later times some will desert the faith and occupy themselves with deceiving spirits and demonic teachings" (1Ti 4:1 ᴺᴱᵀ). Those who do not want to know the truth are easily deceived into believing lies.

Fourth, as unbelievers we too were "serving various lusts and pleasures." The word serving means "to be enslaved" to "various" (or "all sorts of") "lusts and pleasures." The unbeliever chooses to sin because his make up or human (fallen) nature is attracted to "lusts" (Gk., "desires, longings or cravings, especially what is forbidden").

Likewise, the unbeliever pursues "pleasures" (*hedone*, sensual and self-satisfying or gratifying enjoyment) for purely selfish and sinful reasons that he believes will be fulfilling and give some meaning to life. The unsaved are "lovers of pleasure rather than lovers of God" (2 Tim 3:4).

Fifth, we were "living in malice" (kakia, "evil desire to injure") to get even with someone, usually to seek a form of vengeance. This term is used in other lists of vices (Rom 1:29; Eph 4:31; Col 3:8; 1 Pet 2:1)

Sixth, as unbelievers we were "living in ... envy" (*phthonos*, "jealousy, or always craving for more, especially what someone else has"). This results in a perpetual sense of dissatisfaction and disillusionment with life. This sin is also used in the lists of vices (Rom 1:29; Gal 5:21; 1 Tim 6:4; 1 Pet 2:1). "It is the grudging spirit that cannot bear to contemplate someone else's prosperity or their success" (Bruce, Galatians, 249).

Seventh, we formerly were "hateful and hating one another," which is a consequence of envy among other motives. Hate is generated by anyone or anything that gets in the way of what we believe to be what we deserve or need for fulfillment or satisfaction.

Hatred is an ugly sin that breeds isolation and evil deeds with bad conse-quences. John describes a number of symptoms of an unsaved person in his first epistle where he repeats four times how unbelievers tend to hate one another (1 Jn 2:9, 11; 3:15; 4:20).

These descriptions are our reality before coming to know Christ, just as they were in the first century. We need to be broken hearted for those engulfed in their snare and do everything possible to lead them to repentance and trust in Christ as their Savior.

(3) Remind them of their salvation (3:4-7)
3:4a "But when the kindness ..."

The third focus of Titus' ministry of remembrance was of their amazing salva-tion. Paul had just given a seven-fold description of the lost, and now he will give a seven-fold description of our present salvation in Christ. These seven aspects are all one sentence in verses 4-7.

First, we must remember that we are saved because of the "kindness ... of God our Savior." "Kindness" is "*chrestotes*," which describes "providing some-thing beneficial to another." His character must become our new character as Jesus commanded, "But love your enemies, and do good, and lend, expecting nothing back. Then your reward will be great, and you will be sons of the Most High, because he is kind to ungrateful and evil people." (Luke 6:35 NET).

3:4b "... and the love of God our Savior toward man appeared,"

Secondly, we must remember the "...love of God our Savior toward man appeared." "Love" here is the word *philanthropia*, "to have affection for mankind" and refers to compassions and eagerness to alleviate pain, trouble or danger. It always finds a way to be helpful.

This is a common characteristic of God as He has revealed Himself to men, as in Psalms, "But you, O Lord, are a compassionate and merciful God. You are patient and demonstrate great loyal love and faithfulness." (Psa 86:15 NET).

Titus 3:3-4 are similar to Ephesians 2:3-4 where Paul described God's redeem work for those who "formerly lived in the lusts of [their] flesh" (Eph 2:3), but God is described as "rich in mercy because of his great love with which he loved us" (Eph 2:4).

Reflection: If God the Father is described as acting out of His "kindness and love toward mankind," how, then, should we live and relate to even the worst of the world? Describe what this attitude could mean in specific situations.

Salvation by grace

3:5a "not by works of righteousness, which we have done, but according to His mercy He saved us"

Thirdly, we must be reminded that our salvation cannot be achieved by any self-effort or personal merit by good deeds, as Paul wrote, "not by works of righteousness which we have done, but according to His mercy He saved us."

The surest sign that a person is lost and totally ignorant of the truth of the gospel is when he believes his "good" will out-weigh his "bad" and thus be acceptable. Those who think he is not guilty of sin "deceives [himself] and the truth is not in [him]." (1 John 1:8).

The word "saved" (*sozo*) can be physical or spiritual deliverance, depending on the context. The aorist tense implies an action that is complete in the past and not an ongoing process.

Paul's own testimony was to "be found in Him, not having my own righteous-ness, which is from the law, but that which is through faith in Christ, the righteousness which is from God by faith" (Phil 3:9).

Biblically, we are saved from some things and saved for other things. We are saved from the guilt and penalty of sin, (i.e., God's wrath, spiritual death and ultimately hell). We are saved for being "made alive together with Christ" (Eph 2:5); for being transferred "from the domain of darkness, and transferred... to the kingdom of His beloved Son" (Col 1:13) and a multitude of other purposes and privileges.

For clarity, we are reminded that this salvation is not because of anything we have done or could do to merit His gracious offer. Paul described the means for granting us this salvation in Ephesians 2:8-9, "For by grace you have been saved through faith, and that not of yourselves; it is the gift of God, 9 not of works, lest anyone should boast."

Our lives are so tainted with sin that even what we think is our righteousness is unacceptable for God to grant us salvation. Isaiah gave a frank description of our reality when he wrote, "all our so-called righteous acts are like a menstrual rag in your sight. We all wither like a leaf; our sins carry us away like the wind. (Isa 64:6 NET). No wonder we have no option but to depend upon His mercy.

Grace is the attribute of God that motivates Him to grant to the most undeserving sinner absolute forgiveness and cleansing. We could never do anything to deserve His full and unconditional acceptance. The measure of His grace is determined by how much He hates and detests sin, yet is willing to grant us mercy and love when we could never deserve it. Absolutely amazing!

Reflection: Can you put it in your own words why the only way we can be saved is by grace through faith?

Regeneration
3:5c, "through the washing of regeneration"

Fourthly, having demonstrated the "why" of our salvation, now Paul explains the "how" of our new life in Christ. Something marvelous happens within the believing sinner as he/she is saved by His mercy and grace through faith, the "washing of regeneration" that Paul explained "by the washing of water with the word" (Eph. 5:26).

This is not a reference to water baptism, but an allegory depicting total cleansing regeneration through the application of God's promises. Peter reminds us that we "have been born again not of seed which is perishable but imperishable, that is, through the living and abiding word of God"(1 Pet. 1:23).

3:5d *"and renewing of the Holy Spirit,"*

Fifthly, we are to be reminded that our salvation came through this "renewing of the Holy Spirit," (*anakainosis*, "a renovation which makes a person different than in the past" or "to make new"). This is the birthing of the living presence of the Holy Spirit within the new believer from the moment of he begins to trust in Christ as Savior. "If any man is in Christ" (because Christ is in him) "the old things passed away; behold, all things have become new" (2 Cor 5:17).

Greek scholar William Mounce wrote, "The context in Titus 3:5 requires that it be a once-for-all renewal because salvation is seen as an accomplished fact." (Mounce 2000, 449).
The believer is now bonded together with Christ through the Holy Spirit.

Jesus said, "I tell you the solemn truth, unless a person is born from above, he cannot see the kingdom of God." (John 3:3 NET). To be "born again" or "from above" refers to a new regeneration of life in the interior of the repentant sinner.

The "renewing of the Holy Spirit" refers to the implanting of the Holy Spirit inside every believer at the moment of their trusting with all their heart in Christ (Rom 10:9).

This renewal or implanting of the Spirit of God within the believer (Rom 8:9) is the meaning of the phrase "in Christ" (used 76 times in the NT) and the phrase "in Him" (used 46 times) to describe how the believer is inseparable joined to Christ through the new birthing of the Spirit with him (1 John 4:13), Who now dwells permanently within him (1 Tim 1:14).

Reflection: How is this discussion illustrated by the concept of our bodies being a "temple" in 1 Cor 3:16? What do you think is the significance of this reality in our life?

3:6a "whom He poured out on us abundantly ..."

Furthermore, the Father not only saved us by grace through faith and cleansed us from all sin to be acceptable in His sight, but He regenerated us by implanting the Holy Spirit within us generating a new kind of powerful life. He "poured out on us abundantly" His Spirit.

The verb "poured out" (*ekcheo*) is in the aorist tense meaning a single completed past action, not a continuous progressive action. This describes the individual's reception of the Holy Spirit in all His fullness, thus enabling us to "be partakers of the divine nature" (2 Pet 1:4).

The "pouring out" of the Spirit is an integral part of our salvation that produces our "new life" or "regeneration" by the indwelling of the Spirit. This operation of God is called the "baptism of the Spirit" in 1 Cor 12:13, "For by one Spirit we were all baptized into one body-- whether Jews or Greeks, whether slaves or free-- and have all been made to drink into one Spirit." (1Co 12:13).
The verb "baptized" also in the aorist tense, that is, the baptism of the Spirit is a one-time action in the past when all believers are regenerated or born-again (John 3:3).

Paul describes this baptism of the Spirit in 1 Cor 12:13. For in one Spirit we were all baptized into one body. (1Co 12:13 NET). The word "baptized" is a transliteration (not translation) of the word baptize, which means "to immerse, to submerge" into something. At the time of the early translations immersion was not the mode of Christian baptism, so the word was not translated, but transliterated to avoid contradiction.

Water baptism depicts the Spirit baptism by which we are "put into or immersed into" the "one body" of Christ in His death, burial and resurrection.

The Spirit baptism is the operation God accomplished the moment we put our trust in Christ and His Word. The verb form is aorist meaning a past-completed action that occurs once in every believer's experience and never repeated. Once we are "put into" Christ by the Spirit baptism we are all immediately anointed, sealed by the Spirit, and "given us the Spirit in our hearts as a guarantee" (2Co 1:21-22).

Paul described the chronology or sequence of these instantaneous events as, "In Him you also trusted, after you heard the word of truth, the gospel of your salvation; in whom also, having believed, you were sealed with the Holy Spirit of promise, (Eph 1:13).

All of the outpouring, indwelling, sealing of the Spirit occurred at the moment of our salvation when we passed from death to life. This is not a second work of grace or an experience after salvation, nor is it ever repeated as some teach. It is the integral concept of our salvation whereby we are forever united to Christ.

God now lives within us in the presence of the Spirit empowering us to live in His will. The Lord "is able to do exceeding abundantly beyond all that we ask or think, according to the power [i.e., of His Holy Spirit] that works within us" (Eph. 3:20). Because of that available power in us, we are commanded to "be filled with the Spirit" (Eph. 5:18) as we walk in His will.

In Titus 3:6 the adverb "abundantly" is a further explanation of the work of God accomplished at the moment of our salvation.

 The Holy Spirit is given "abundantly" (*plousios*, "richly, exceedingly, excessively"), that is, at the new birth the Spirit is given in His fullness, without reserve. Paul described this new relationship as, "For in him all the fullness of deity lives in bodily form, and you have been filled in him, who is the head over every ruler and authority." (Col 2:9-10 NET).

3:6b "...through Jesus Christ our Savior"
Sixth, we must remember that our salvation can only come through the substitutionary and atoning sacrifice of God's Son, "Jesus Christ our Savior," because God is just, so sin can only be justly punished through the death and shedding of blood (Heb 9:22). This cruel act depicts how horrible our sins are to our holy God.

To be able to forgive sinners, a perfect innocent substitute must receive the guilt of our sins, then suffer the just wrath for our sins. Paul described it, "For He made Him who knew no sin to be sin for us, that we might become the righteousness of God in Him." (2Co 5:21). This was God's gracious plan from eternity past.

Reflection: Isn't this amazing? We could never deserve such benefits of His grace. How does this make you feel about your salvation?

The purpose of it all
3:7 "that having been justified by His grace we should become heirs according

to the hope of eternal life."

The seventh aspect that we need to be constantly reminded of is the resulting justification "by His grace" in order to "become heirs according to the hope of eternal life." This is another purpose clause introduced by *hina* in Greek. Having accepted God's grace in sending Christ to take all the wrath of God for our sins, we have "been justified by His grace" (another aorist verb that refers to a past fully completed action that cannot be added to, changed or repeated).

The idea of being "justified" is an act of God whereby our sins become Christ's and His righteousness becomes ours (2 Cor 5:21). "Justification" describes deliverance from the curse of sin, because that curse was placed on Christ (Gal 3:11-13) and now He can declare us "righteous." Paul never got over this display of grace as when he wrote, "to the praise of the glory of His grace, by which He has made us accepted in the Beloved. (Eph 1:6).

As a result of "having been justified" and indwelt with the Spirit, now "The Spirit himself bears witness to our spirit that we are God's children." (Rom 8:16 NET) Thus accepted as a "child of God" the result is "then heirs-- heirs of God and joint heirs with Christ" (Rom 8:17). Joint-heirs to the inheritance of Jesus Christ is no small thing.

Peter was enthusiastic because of this promise: ""Blessed be the God and Father of our Lord Jesus Christ, who according to His great mercy has caused us to be born again to a living hope through the resurrection of Jesus Christ from the dead, to obtain an inheritance which is imperishable and undefiled and will not fade away, reserved in heaven" (1 Pet. 1:3–4).

Reflection: Can you begin to see why Paul was so protective of a true and clear understanding of this comprehensive salvation? Is there any part that needs further discussion or clarification? This is the "richness" of His grace mentioned 44 times in the NT.

(4) Remind them of their mission (3:8)

3:8 "This is a faithful saying, and these things I want you to affirm constantly, that those who have believed in God should be careful to maintain good works.

These things are good and profitable to men."

Titus had to remind the believers on Crete of a fourth concept that was critical to the task of reaching out to their pagan society. They could not stop talking about or "affirm constantly" the message of this Book of Titus. The affirmations to reiterate were all "these things" discussed especially in this chapter, but extend to the whole Book. People tend to forget important truths and need to be reminded constantly.

"These things" refers most directly to the preceding concepts: (1) the kindness of the Father and His love for mankind; (2) the work of the Holy Spirit in regenerating and empowering man; (3) the grace of Jesus Christ Who caused our justification by giving us freely His righteousness; (4) the purpose of making all believers to become heirs of eternal life with Christ. This is the gospel story, as Paul explains it.

The key responsibility of reiterating these truths is explained as for all "those who have believed God" (a past completed action with present effect) and refers to those who have taken God at His word to be saved through His grace without any works of personal righteousness. However, now these believers are to "be careful to maintain good works" not so they can be saved, accepted or even secure in their salvation, but so outsiders can benefit from their actions and be drawn to Christ. As they have received grace, now they are to show grace to others, especially to unbelievers.

They are to do holistic actions that "are good and profitable to men" in general. Holistic means that their actions are both physical, emotional and spiritual: caring for the whole person.

These actions can be a variety of things from prayer for others to granting physical or monetary aid to anyone in need within your sphere of influence. Jesus taught this life principal, "In the same way, let your light shine before people, so that they can see your good deeds and give honor to your Father in heaven." (Mat 5:16 NET).

Jesus is the "light of the world" (John 8:12; 9:5) that shines as we tell the gospel story, then listeners look closer to see if the gospel made any difference in the speaker's life and discover a wealth of "good deeds." Their response should be to "honor" God by recognizing the truth or genuineness of the transforming power of the Light. The objective is to attract people to the Light of the world.

Final directives to the church

God's plan is designed to reproduce healthy churches that know and live out the transforming power of the gospel in the life of every believer. Leaders are to be examples of this transformed life (chapter 1) and together we are to help each other grow in maturity with a purpose of reflecting the life of Christ within us (chapter 2), then believers are to clarify the gospel to the unsaved world while demonstrating Christ-like care for others.

Paul concludes his epistle with instructions in four areas of the ministry. They concern relationships with (1) false teachers, (2) divisive people within the church, (3) co-laborers and (4) his faithful friends.

1. Arguing with False Teachers

3:9 "But avoid~~ foolish disputes, genealogies, contentions, and strivings about the law; for they are unprofitable and useless."

The believers and churches on Crete had heard many itinerating teachers (as was the custom of the early church) who brought confusion and contradictory views.

Titus was to appoint leaders who would "Hold fast the pattern of sound words which you have heard from me, in faith and love which are in Christ Jesus. (2 Tim 1:13) and "will be able to give exhortation in such healthy teaching and correct those who speak against it." (Tit 1:9)

This was a large group of "many insubordinate, both idle talkers and deceivers" (1:10). They were distorting the gospel message by telling "myths" and stories that could not be confirmed (likely miraculous stories to prove their spirituality) and dangerous legalistic tendencies ("commandments of men" – 1:14).

These false teachers professed "to know God, but by their deeds they deny Him, being detestable and disobedient, and worthless for any good deed" (1:16).

The command "avoid" in the progressive present tense means to be "continually avoiding." The verb *periistemi* means to "step around so as to avoid." These issues are to be "shunned" or to "go around" them. By their self-seeking lifestyle false teachers were hindering the credibility of the gospel.

Anyone who teaches contrary to Paul's teachings and "does not agree with sound words (that is, those of our Lord Jesus Christ) and with the teaching that accords with godliness," (1Ti 6:3 NET) then they must be avoided because "he is conceited and understands nothing, but has an unhealthy interest in controversies and verbal disputes.

This gives rise to envy, dissension, slanders, evil suspicions" (1Tim 6:4 NET).

Paul gives four areas of their false teachings to avoid:

> a) Foolish disputes or controversies
> b) Genealogies
> c) Contentions or strife
> d) Disputes about the law

1) *Foolish controversies* were common in the Early Church because the Apostles were few and the written Scriptures were not complete and copies were scarce. In the church at Ephesus Timothy was facing similar problems and was told to "instruct certain men not to teach strange doctrines, nor to pay attention to myths and endless genealogies, which give rise to mere speculation rather than furthering the administration of God which is by faith." (1Ti 1:3-4 NAS)

The danger of these false ideas is that they distract from the written Word of God. The fabulous stories, amazing experiences, new ideas or doctrines and logical conclusions from misapplied Bible texts appeal to those Christians who are poorly trained in God's Word. "For some men, straying from these things, have turned aside to fruitless discussion" (1Ti 1:6 NAS).

Some discussions that are not based on understanding biblical truths are useless. Arguing over validity of experiences, dreams, revelations and philosophical logic or arguments that define doctrine are seldom profitable because they are biblically not provable.

Interpretations of genealogies using the allegorical interpretations or numerology for gleaning some spiritual or prophetical meaning from lists of names in the Bible or contemporary names has fascinated Jews for centuries.

This could also refer to special religious or spiritual significance because of being descendants of certain persons. The general rule is that anything drawing one's attention from the primary and simple meaning of the biblical text is destructive speculation.

Strife or contentions refers to rivalry and antagonistic groups that breed discord, judging and rejection of each other, quarreling and division. It quenches love, acceptance and care for one another in the church. The Greek words for quarrel or contentions and the word for sword are derived from the same root. Striving about the law, that is, the Mosaic law, which is likely a result of some converted Jews within the church who ignored or rejected the conclusion of the Jerusalem Council (AD 49 in Acts 15).

These "strivings" translate *mache* meaning "fighting and quarrels" that tend to be intense and bitter. These disputes persist today in the form of some cults or sects that insist on applying the OT Mosaic law to the contemporary church.

These are to be avoided because they are "unprofitable and useless," because they are "of no advantage," usually "fantastic stories" or fanciful interpretations (i.e., conclusions from numerology) that can be impressive, but are pure imagination that distract from a true analysis of God's Word.

Paul warned of a time when this would be common: "For there will be a time when people will not tolerate sound teaching. Instead, following their own desires, they will accumulate teachers for themselves, because they have an insatiable curiosity to hear new things. 4 And they will turn away from hearing the truth, but on the other hand they will turn aside to myths." (2Tim 4:3 NET).

Each of these four errors is referred to in 1 Timothy and two are mentioned in

2 Timothy. These appear to be the same problem in the church at Ephesus (Timothy's charge) that are confronted by all three letters (Titus, 1 & 2 Timothy). We are not told the specifics of the error, rather the kinds of issues to avoid in the churches.

Reflection: Why would you suspect that there is such an attraction to the controversial, speculative and imaginary interpretations? Can you think of any that you have heard of today?

What does Paul mean when he says these arguments are "unprofitable and useless?"

3:10-11 "Reject~~ a divisive man after the first and second admonition,"

Generally, the ideas to be avoided are promoted by individual(s) that pretend to have a fresh revelation or unique insight. The command "reject" in the present tense means "to continually have nothing to do with someone or avoid any association with" such a person.

The word for "divisive man" is *hairetikos* (from which we get the word heretic) means someone who is "choosing for himself or personal opinion," as opposed to follow the authority of another. It came to mean someone who placed his personal opinions above the truth of God's word, while refusing to consider any viewpoint but his own.

This meaning gave rise to another, namely, "a set of persons professing certain definite principles or opinions," hence a school or party; for example, the "party of the Sadducees" (Acts 5:17), and "the party of the Pharisees" (Acts 15:5; cf. 26:5)… It is true, of course, that the term as here used need not be restricted to a particular type of fanatic. Every factious person stands condemned here.

The word is listed in association with grave "deeds of the flesh" such as "immorality, impurity, sensuality, idolatry, sorcery, enmities, strife, jealousy, outbursts of anger, disputes, dissensions, factions, envying, drunkenness, carousing" (Gal. 5:19–21).

This person believes he is the final authority and everyone must submit to his ideas. Typically he is insubordinate, critical, judgmental of every other leader and constantly voicing his contrary opinions.

It seems that most churches in the NT had some of these divisive persons. The Roman church was no exception: "Now I urge you, brothers and sisters, to watch out for those who create dissensions and obstacles contrary to the teaching that you learned. Avoid them! For these are the kind who do not serve our Lord Christ, but their own appetites. By their smooth talk and flattery they deceive the minds of the naive." (Rom 16:17-18 NET).

Again in the Thessalonian church, "But if anyone does not obey our message through this letter, take note of him and do not associate closely with him, so that he may be ashamed. Yet do not regard him as an enemy, but admonish him as a brother." (2Thess 3:14-15 NET)

Reflective: Have you ever heard of or been a part of a church split? What was the cause? What should have been done to help resolve the issue?
When a divisive spirit is noted the leader is to follow the steps that Jesus taught for resolving conflicts in the church (Mat 18:15-16), where the first admonition is private, then the second admonition is with two or three witnesses.

Depending on the nature of the divisive ideas, the first admonitions should be "with gentleness correcting those who are in opposition, if perhaps God may grant them repentance leading to the knowledge of the truth" (2 Tim. 2:25).

If a spirit of rebellion is dominant and there is no repentance, then according to Matt 18:17, he is to be avoided and shunned and the church notified that this person is not treated as a part of the body of the church any longer.

By his reaction to the exhortation and admonition the person reveals, "that such a person is warped and sinning, being self-condemned." (Tit 3:11) The symptom of a fool is indicated by how he responds to correction (Prov 15:5).

Unfortunately some leaders in evangelical churches teach ideas that are unrelated or contrary to Scripture, but are often not disciplined, rather are given opportunities to promote their erroneous views, often because they are popular among the audience.

One of the core characteristics of a church is the overwhelming sense of peace among the brethren; that is, all issues are resolved (Col 3:12-13) and they let nothing interfere with letting "the peace of God rule in your hearts" (the use of the plural commands implies that the meaning is for the whole church, not primarily to individuals).

If we hope to have an impact on our community we need to demonstrate our bond of love for one another. The Lord told the Twelve, "By this all men will know that you are My disciples, if you have love for one another" (John 13:35). Paul expressed this unity as "Let nothing be done through selfish ambition or conceit, but in lowliness of mind let each esteem others better than himself." (Phi 2:3).

Reflection: What kind of things can disrupt the "peace of God" among the believers in churches that you know?

3:11 "…knowing that such a person is warped and sinning, being self-condemned."

Any Christian that is confronted with their disobedience, rebellion or problem causing among the church should always respond quickly to correction. To persist in stubborn ways is symptomatic of deeper problems. Such a person is "warped" (Gk., "twisted, distorted, perverted"); that is, he is not seeing or living "straight."

God puts spiritual leaders into our lives who "watch out for your souls," so we are to "obey those who rule over you and be submissive" (Heb 13:17). When confronted a child of God must respond humbly and with repentance.

What makes this person's sin so grave is that he knows he is sinning both from conscience and the two-fold warnings, thus his reaction only reveal "being self-condemned" (3:11). Such confrontational corrections should never be motivated from a vendetta or desire to get rid of someone; rather, every effort should be extended to winning the erring person into harmony with the church.

Reflection: What issues would you think should merit this type of intervention?

Treating of fellow servants

3:12 "When I send Artemas to you, or Tychicus, be diligent to come to me at Nicopolis, for I have decided to spend the winter there."

In a final personal word to Titus Paul describes how he is making plans to rendezvous to spend the winter together in Nicopolis, about two hundred miles northwest of Athens on the west coast of Greece.

First, the churches are not to be left without supervision and/or leadership, so he is sending Artemas or Tychicus to take Titus' place before he leaves to join Paul in Nicopolis.

Paul apparently is elsewhere, likely in Macedonia confirming the churches from which he writes this epistle. When he says, "I have decided to spend the winter there," implies that he is somewhere else, or he would have said, "here." Winter was not a time for traveling in the Mediterranean Sea (Acts 27:12; 28:11; 1 Cor 16:6 and 2 Tim 4:21).

It seems Titus reached Nicopolis, then did some evangelistic work in Dalmatia (just up the coast from Nicopolis), then returned there later (1 Tim 4:9-10). The move to Nicopolis puts Paul's gospel ministry one step further west than the team had gone before. This point was also an ideal jumping off place for a trip to Spain, which had been his original objective (Rom 15:20-24).

We do not know anything about Artemas except that Paul had great confidence in his ability to practice and implement the content of his letter to Titus in the Cretan churches.

Tychicus is mentioned a number of times in the NT as a companion of Paul on his journey from Corinth to Asia Minor (Acts 20:4). He delivered Paul's letter to the church at Colossae (Col 4:7) and Ephesus (Eph 6:21). He is described as "my dear brother and faithful servant in the Lord" (Eph 6:21 NET). It is likely that Paul had sent Tychicus to replace Timothy in Ephesus (2 Tim 4:12), such that now Paul is sending Artemas to replace Titus on Crete.

Reflection: What are some lessons about leadership, ministry and strategy can you derive from this verse?

3:14a "Send*~ Zenas the lawyer and Apollos ..."

Paul makes one other request to Titus before he leaves Crete. He is to "Send Zenas the lawyer and Apollos on their journey with haste, that they may lack nothing. (Tit 3:13). The verb means "to accompany, escort or assist someone in making a journey with food, money, by arranging for companions, means of travel, etc." (BDAG).

We know nothing about "Zenas the lawyer" except what is implied by being a partner with Apollos, the great Jewish Christian orator, who "was mighty in the Scriptures" (Acts 18:24). Though he had "been instructed in the way of the Lord," and was "fervent in spirit, he was speaking and teaching accurately the things concerning Jesus" (Acts 18:24-25[NAS]), but he was not completely accurate in his interpretation. "But when Priscilla and Aquila heard him, they took him aside and explained to him the way of God more accurately." (Act 18:26 [NAS]).

Here is a great preacher who needed exhorting and correcting by some of Paul's disciples, Priscilla and Aquila. He evidently responded positively and with gratitude, later leaving Corinth to return to Ephesus (1 Cor 16:12).

Reflection: Have you ever been corrected for what you did, taught or believed by someone who knew the Scripture? How did you feel? How did you respond?

Missionary support precedence
3:14b "Send... on their journey with haste, that they may lack nothing."

Paul wanted to set a precedence for the treatment of itinerating teachers in the

Early Church so Titus was to help them "on their way so that nothing is lacking for them" (Titus 3:13).

The key to the expansion of the church and the gospel was the ability of itinerating teachers/preachers to build up the exploding house churches (Rom 16:5; 1 Cor 16:19; Col 4:15; Phm 1:2), often traveling with their wives (and families?) (1 Cor 9:5). Expenses were inevitable. The churches were to facilitate these physical needs as the teachers provided "spiritual things" (1 Cor 9:11).

Reflection: Have can you help missionaries continue their ministry by supporting them? Who could you help?

The final charge
3:14 "And let our people also learn~~ to maintain good works, to meet urgent needs, that they may not be unfruitful."

The surface reading may miss the imperative verb, that is, a command for the church, "our people" who were to "keep on learning how to maintain good works" (sense of present tense imperative). There are always new opportunities and new needs to be learning how to meet.

Titus could not do it all. Everyone had to play a part in supporting the ministry leaders. This was to be "learned" just like doctrine, meaning of the Scriptures and how to live. They were to learn how they should sacrifice for the ministry by maintaining "good works to meet urgent needs." This is a self-education that springs out of the biblical principle of serving Christ, through serving others (Matt 25:40,45).

The final purpose clause (*hina*) suggests that the believer does not want to be "unfruitful." Jesus marked the difference among those who heard the gospel in four categories. The third group is defined as "Now he who received seed among the thorns is he who hears the word, and the cares of this world and the deceitfulness of riches choke the word, and he becomes unfruitful." (Mat 13:22).

Peter described the pattern of the Christian life as "diligently adding to your faith" and he concludes saying, "For if these things are yours and abound, you will be neither barren nor unfruitful in the knowledge of our Lord Jesus Christ. (2 Pet 1:8).

Preaching is not the only way to be fruitful, but facilitating the expansion of the ministry by helping missionaries and evangelists God weighs our sacrifice as participating in the ministry of another. "The author of this epistle realizes fully that though grace is the root (Titus 3:7; cf. Eph. 2:8), noble deeds are the fruit (cf. Eph. 2:10) of the tree of salvation."

In the context of the Philippian church contributing to Paul and his team of co-workers he thanked the church for their help and gave them a suggestion of a future reward: "Not that I seek the gift, but I seek the fruit that abounds to your account." (Phil 4:17).

Nothing is missed by God. "Therefore, my beloved brethren, be steadfast, immovable, always abounding in the work of the Lord, knowing that your labor is not in vain in the Lord." (1Co 15:58) He keeps perfect records of every effort done for His kingdom and His honor.

Reflection: Do you pray to be "fruitful" for Christ's kingdom? Discuss how to do different projects or "good deeds" that could have an impact on the world?

3:15 "All who are with me greet you. Greet~~ those who love us in the faith. Grace be with you all. Amen."

Paul sends his greetings from his entire team, an unnamed team in Macedonia. He then gives one last command: "Greet those who love [phileo] us in the faith." There was an apparent deep affection for fellow believers in the Early Church. To love Paul meant to love "the faith" he revealed in the Scriptures he wrote by inspiration, and taught to the churches, especially in this epistle to Titus, which was soon to be made public for all the churches.

"Grace be with you all," that is, God's favor in Christ from those who do not deserve it," was extended beyond Titus, as the plural "you all" suggests. The implied intent of the epistle was meant to be for the entire Cretan church and others until today.

Reflection: Do you love those who love the Word of God and His global purpose in the world today? Be sure to constantly greet them and become a partner with them.

Bibliography

Alford, H. (2010). Alford's Greek Testament: an exegetical and critical commentary. Bellingham, WA: Logos Bible Software.

Barton, B. B., Veerman, D., & Wilson, N. S. (1993). 1 Timothy, 2 Timothy, Titus. Wheaton, IL: Tyndale House Publishers.

Bauer, W., (1979). A Greek-English Lexicon of the New Testament and Other Early Christian Literature, tr. W. F. Arndt and F. W. Gingrich. 2nd ed. rev. and augmented by F. W. Gingrich and F. W. Danker from Bauer's 5th ed. (1958), Chicago.

Biblical Studies Press. (2006). The NET Bible First Edition Notes. Biblical Studies Press.

Carson, D. A., France, R. T., Motyer, J. A., & Wenham, G. J. (Eds.). (1994). New Bible commentary: 21st century edition (4th ed.). Leicester, England; Downers Grove, IL: Inter-Varsity Press.

Hendriksen, W., & Kistemaker, S. J. (1953–2001). Exposition of the Pastoral Epistles (Grand Rapids: Baker Book House.). Vol. 4.

Knight, G. W. (1992). The Pastoral Epistles: a commentary on the Greek text (p. 307). Grand Rapids, MI; Carlisle, England: W.B. Eerdmans; Paternoster Press.

Lea, T. D., & Griffin, H. P. (1992). 1, 2 Timothy, Titus (Vol. 34, p. 299). Nashville: Broadman & Holman Publishers.

MacArthur, J. F., Jr. (1996). Titus, Chicago: Moody Press,

MacDonald, W. (1995). Believer's Bible Commentary: Old and New Testaments. (A. Farstad, Ed.). Nashville: Thomas Nelson.

Metzger, B. M., United Bible Societies. (1994). A textual commentary on the Greek New Testament, second edition a companion volume to the United Bible Societies' Greek New Testament (4th rev. ed.). London; New York: United Bible Societies.

Mounce, W. D. (2000). Pastoral Epistles. vol. 46. Dallas: Word, Incorporated.

Nicoll, W. R. (n.d.). The expositor's Greek Testament: Commentary (Vol. 4). New York: George H. Doran Company.

Pelikan, J. ed. (1966) (Luther's Works. St. Louis: Concordia.

Staton, K. (1988). Timothy–Philemon: Unlocking the Scriptures for You. Cincinnati, OH: Standard.

Walvoord, John F., & Zuck, R. B., Dallas Theological Seminary. (1985). The

Bible Knowledge Commentary: An Exposition of the Scriptures. Wheaton, IL: Victor Books.

Zerwick, M., & Grosvenor, M. (1974). A grammatical analysis of the Greek New Testament. Rome: Biblical Institute Press.

www.ingramcontent.com/pod-product-compliance
Lightning Source LLC
Chambersburg PA
CBHW071641050426
42443CB00026B/801